CHILDHOOD OF WORLD FIGURES

CHRISTOPHER COLUMBUS

YOUNG EXPLORER

By Kathleen Kudlinski

D0819321

Aladdin Paperbacks
New York   London   Toronto   Sydney

❧ ALADDIN PAPERBACKS
An imprint of Simon & Schuster Children's Publishing Division
1230 Avenue of the Americas, New York, NY 10020
Text copyright © 2005 by Kathleen Kudlinski
All rights reserved, including the right of
reproduction in whole or in part in any form.
ALADDIN PAPERBACKS and colophon are registered
trademarks of Simon & Schuster, Inc.
Designed by Lisa Vega
The text of this book was set in Aldine721 BT.
Manufactured in the United States of America
First Aladdin Paperbacks edition March 2005
10 9 8 7 6 5 4 3 2 1
Library of Congress Control Number 2004108146
ISBN 0-689-87648-3

To you, if you are bilingual.

You are smart and lucky, too.

You are ready to explore

and understand two cultures.

CONTENTS

Christopher Columbus's childhood is a mystery. Records show that he was born in the Italian city-state of Genoa in 1451, sometime in the fall. His parents, Domenico and Susanna Columbus, were both master wool weavers. Red-haired "Cristoforo Colombo" (Christopher Columbus's name in Italian) spent hours every day working in his parents' shop. Even with his help, the weavers were sometimes in debt. We know that by Cristoforo's late teens, he and his younger brother Bartolo decided to leave the family business. In medieval Genoa, it could have happened like this. . . .

★ ★ ★

CHAPTER ONE
BAAAA

"Make haste, Cris!"

"Bartolo Colombo, you stop there," Cristoforo scolded his brother. "We have time to watch the boats before Mama needs us." He shaded his eyes against the summer sun. "See the ship entering our harbor, Barti? 'Tis a caravel. 'Tis smaller and faster than the bigger boats. That triangle sail is light and easy to—"

"Tri . . . ?" Bartolo sounded out the word. "She wears a Trinity sail?"

Cristoforo laughed at the mistake, but he crossed himself quickly and glanced around the dock. Using a holy word in a joke could get them in trouble with the priest—or with God.

Sailors, townspeople, and slaves worked, hauling bales and casks from the ships tied along the dock. No one had heard Bartolo's idle blasphemy. "Look closely, Barti," Cristoforo said. "A 'triangular' sail has three points, not four, like the square ones. 'Tis called a lateen sail."

"You know everything about boats, Cris," Bartolo said. "When I get to be the older one, will I know more than you?"

Cristoforo hid his smile. "When you have had nine saint's days, as I have, you will be as old as I am. But"—he paused—"by then, I will be older still. I will always be almost three years older. And smarter by far."

"'Tis not fair," Bartolo grumbled. Cristoforo bent to pull his brother's legging up over his knee and retied it to strings on the boy's vest. "Who is yon boy?" Bartolo asked, pointing at a stranger. "He looks old. He will always be older even than you, Cris, won't he? And smarter still?"

Cristoforo gazed across the dock at a stranger sitting cross-legged atop a barrel, tying knots in a rope. The boy's filthy doublet was woven as finely as anything from the Colombo looms. The loose-sleeved shirt beneath was well made too. The stranger wore ripped, graying hose, and his hair was tied into a pig's tail behind his head. "He's just a cabin boy, Barti," Cristoforo told his brother. "And by the looks of him, he is not a day older than me—and never will be."

The young sailor stared at the Colombos as they turned toward home. "What are you looking at?" Cristoforo challenged.

"Your hair, sir," the stranger called. "'Tis almost as red as your nose, or those lovely soft hands."

Cristoforo felt his face flush. "What of it?"

"You look out of place in sorry little Genoa. I have seen people colored like you before—red hair, pale eyes and skin—but not in all of the Republics of Italy. Or in Portugal, either. Or Spain."

"Where, then, pray tell?" Cristoforo demanded. Bartolo stepped behind him.

The cabin boy jumped off the barrel and swaggered across the dock. "'Twas on my first voyage on the Ocean Sea."

Cristoforo drew a breath. The Ocean Sea? Even his father had never gone that far to trade their cloths and clothing.

"Aye," the boy went on. "We sailed for near a year, past the truly great ports. Any of them makes this village seem backward."

Cristoforo felt his fists clench. *Lovely, soft hands?* All of the sailor's words stung. "Genoa is surely the greatest city in the world," he said.

"We visited fair Barcelona," the cabin boy said, ignoring him. "Then we skimmed past Moorish Granada, where the Moslem ships rule the waters, dropped anchor in Lisbon, and then sailed onward." He paused and turned to stare up at the arches on a row of huge marble buildings ringing the harbor. Beyond them, hundreds of homes and shops climbed the steep hills toward the watchtowers on the hilltops. Gardens and cathedral spires, workshops and guildhalls all showed the wealth of Genoa.

A backward village? Cristoforo wanted to turn on his heel at the insult, but first he had to ask, "Where did you see other redheads?"

"For weeks," the cabin boy went on smugly, "we sailed north, to a land cold and strange and a port called Bristol in a place called England." He paused again and took his time, picking his teeth. Cristoforo made himself wait silently while Bartolo pulled at his hand.

"Cris has been to all those places too," the little boy interrupted. "Cris has seen everything!"

Cristoforo shook his head at his brother. The last thing he wanted to do was admit that he had never stepped past the borders of the Republic of Genoa.

"Beyond that," the cabin boy was talking to Bartolo now, "we went north again, to a distant land where many people had hair as red as your brother's. But they did not all stink so much of sheep." He sniffed as delicately as if he were the king of Spain.

"Who smells like sheep?" Cristoforo said.

Beside him, Bartolo said, "Baaaa-baaa."

"You both smell," the cabin boy said. "I would guess you spent half the morn rolling in raw lamb's fleece. Is that the only entertainment in this sorry little village?"

Cristoforo looked down, then tried to brush off the tufts of wool caught in the pleats and folds of his clothing. *There are plays and fine concerts here,* he thought furiously. The Genoa market was full of jesters and jugglers, the gallows, and even a puppet theater.

"Little one, you are so good with your lamb's call," the stranger taunted Bartolo. "Give it again. Loud enough so all can hear."

Bartolo took a deep breath and "Baaa-ed" at the top of his lungs. Men nearby turned to look and began laughing. Cristoforo's face burned. He clapped his hand over his brother's mouth and glared at the newcomer. "Leave him alone!"

"Baaaaaaa backwater simpkin," the cabin boy said, and, "Baaaaaa," until Cristoforo pushed at him.

The boy stepped backward and tripped over a rope, then fell hard on the cobblestones. When Cristoforo reached down to help him up, the boy yelled, "Unhand me!" His voice carried as loud as a church bell at dawn.

Suddenly a large sailor stood beside Cristoforo.

Others drifted toward them. Bartolo's hand found Cristoforo's and clung tightly.

"We have a problem here, young master?" the sailor asked, slowly pulling a long knife from its scabbard. He stared at Cristoforo and the cabin boy.

"Mama!" Bartolo screamed. "Mama!"

"Back off, stranger!" a deep voice boomed. Cristoforo turned to see Master DiCaprio, the chairman of the weavers' guild, striding down the dock. "Only a sorry excuse for a man picks fights with smooth-faced lads." The gold necklace of his guild office glinted in the sun. Behind him, other guildsmen ran from their shops.

More sailors gathered. "Who called this party?" the master weaver demanded.

"You think I am a 'sorry excuse for a man'?" the big sailor bellowed, helping the cabin boy to his feet. The lad stood looking dazed, rubbing at his head. Sailors and guildsmen gestured with knives and fists.

"Dirty sailing scum!" another townsman yelled.

Cristoforo held his breath.

"Father Giovanni!" Bartolo cried beside him.

The yelling ended suddenly as everyone turned to nod in respect to the priest. The Father swept across the dock, robes fluttering. His gaunt face looked furious. Cristoforo wanted to jump into the harbor.

"Who started this melee?" the priest asked, his high voice wavering in the air. When no one answered, the priest demanded, "Step forward, scoundrels, and I will assign penance."

Bartolo stepped first, but Cristoforo pulled him back. "Nay. It was me, Father," he said. He winced, trying to imagine what penalty he would have to pay for breaking the peace of Genoa's waterfront.

"Our young poppin had a hand in it, too," the sailor said, pushing the cabin boy to the front of the crowd.

The priest stared at them while the crowd backed off silently. Cristoforo thought time itself stood still. The sun beat down, gulls mewed in the harbor, and the water *lap-lapped* at the pilings. Bartolo sniffled. "You," the priest said, his hand resting suddenly on Cristoforo's head. "Master weaver's son, have you ever scrubbed a ship's deck, stem to stern? That might just tame your spirit."

The cabin boy snorted in derision beside him. "Silence," the priest snapped. "Young sailor, have *you* ever carded all the wool in a grown sheep's fleece? You could learn a gentler touch with people."

Chuckles began in the crowd around them, then guffaws. "Well done!" someone shouted. "God bless you, Father," another said, and almost everyone made the sign of the cross.

The cabin boy looked furious, but Cristoforo could not stop grinning. At last he would board a ship and work with real sailors!

CHAPTER TWO

SAINT CRISTOFORO'S DAY

Bong! Bing! Bong!

"Cristoforo!" Mama's voice joined the pealing of church bells. "Dress for Mass, boy! 'Tis Saint Cristoforo's Day!"

Cristoforo tried to turn over on the sleeping pallet on the floor and groaned. The muscles of both arms burned as he pulled the fine-spun blanket back over his head. His fingers cramped, remembering the feel of the rough wooden scrub brush. How many hours had he scrubbed at the deck, he wondered? Until his knees were raw and his back muscles had passed from pain into numbness.

But that ship! Cristoforo pulled the blanket down again and smiled out the small-paned window at the blue sky beyond. How good it had felt to be out in the breeze, rocking with the movement of the waters below! The creaking and sighing of the boat timbers had become like a song. When the ropes slapped the mast, they were like drums played by the wind itself. And that air! Out away from the city's open sewers and garbage dumps, the droppings of dog and horse, pig and goat, the breeze was cleaner than Cristoforo had ever smelled it. No wonder, he thought, the cabin boy had noticed the sheep smell clinging to his clothes!

"Cris! Cris!" Bartolo cried, jumping onto Cristoforo's gut.

"Oooooof!" Cristoforo gagged and rolled over. "Go away!"

"May I hold your saint's day coin? Just one time?"

Cristoforo rolled off the pallet and lurched to his feet. This was his day! "You may touch my coin," he told his brother, "*if* I get one this year." There had not always been enough in the shop's till to spare, even on saint's days. Cristoforo threw open the clothes chest. He pulled out his best doublet, the red velvet one embroidered with white and yellow birds. First, he slid one sleeve up over his arm, then tied it on. Then he tied on the other sleeve. His white undershirt bloused through the slashes in the sleeves and puffed out where he tucked the shirttail into his hose.

"Well, are we not the fine little man?" Mama said when she saw him. "You surely have grown since the last time you dressed in finery! When she pursed her lips and whistled at his legs, Cristoforo tried to pull the edges of his doublet down.

Papa laughed. "Almost time to pass that garb down to your baby brother." Bartolo howled in outrage, but Papa stroked his beard, considering. "'Twill last another few months, son. 'Tis the fashion today to bare more leg."

"Not *thy* scrawny old-man legs, Domenico!" Mama said. Papa picked up a ball of yarn and threw it at her.

"If the trade routes would just open again, Signora, I would buy a satin tunic to drag below my knee. And I would dress thee in fine Chinese silks and spread Oriental rugs beneath thy feet. I could weave fabulous cloths and make a king's ransom for my fair lady."

"I will enjoy the dress," Mama answered, "but, ah, the spices! If we could get foreign spices once again, I could make your meals taste fresh, even when they have turned a little bad."

"A *little* bad?" Papa made a ghastly face and grabbed at his gut. "Now that the Moslems block all the trade routes, nothing tastes good."

"Remember cinnamon?" Cristoforo said. His mouth watered at the thought of cakes and fancies.

"And pepper?" Domenico said, and faked a giant sneeze.

"'Tis there no other way to get spice?" Bartolo asked.

"Nay," Papa said. "Henry the Navigator keeps trying to take a boat all around Africa. He thinks he could sail right into the land of monkeys and parrots, ivory, silks, and pepper—"

"And dreams and nonsense," Mama interrupted. "Give the boy his tenth saint's day present and let us be off to the church," she scolded. Papa dug in the shop takings box for a coin and flipped it at Cris. Bartolo looked at him pleadingly. Mama tucked her overskirt up into her waist and whisked out the door. Cris followed, treasuring how cool and hard and strange the coin felt in his hand.

They made it into the church as the bells pealed again. Father Giovanni glared their way, then began reciting the service in Latin. Cristoforo knelt and rose, repeated and crossed himself from memory. Even Papa did not know Latin, Cris thought. That language was only for priests and scholars. On the ship, sailors had spoken in Italian and Portuguese, and some Spanish. They had seemed not to notice him kneeling on the deck, scrub brush in hand. He had heard things said that made him blush, sometimes in anger and sometimes in embarrassment. He knew bawdy jokes, he thought, that Papa would not even know. Not that he would dare tell them to his father.

"Christophorus . . ." Only part of his mind heard the priest. A sharp jab from his mother's elbow helped focus his attention. Cris stood. "Christophorus Columbus," Father Giovanni intoned in Latin. Then he switched into Genovese Italian so all could understand. "Cristoforo Colombo, your namesake calls you to do great things for our Lord. Saint Cristoforo lived hundreds of years ago. He was a huge man, a giant, strong as an ox, and built like a bear. After searching for years to find Jesus, he settled for a life of simple service."

The priest strode down from the altar toward the Colombos and went on: "Saint Cristoforo lived alone in a hut by the shallows of a swift-flowing river. Whenever travelers came to the crossing, he offered to ferry them himself, on his broad shoulders."

Father Giovanni stopped in front of Cristoforo and stared into his eyes as he told the familiar story. "One night, as Saint Cristoforo slept, a tap came at the door, then another. When he roused, it was but a child wanting to cross the river. The saint swept him up on his shoulders."

The priest put his hands on Cristoforo's shoulders and went on. "He grabbed his staff and entered the water. Midstream, the child suddenly became heavy." The Father's hands pressed down. "Cristoforo carried on," the priest continued, pressing ever harder. "His legs began quivering with the effort." Cristoforo himself was having trouble standing under the weight. "His knees began buckling before he reached the far bank," Father Giovanni said, just as Cristoforo's own knees started to give way. "But Cristoforo struggled to get his strange burden to safety." The Father's unflinching stare was all that held Cristoforo up now.

"On dry land again, he gently set the child down." The burden lifted suddenly from Cristoforo's shoulders, and he felt himself rise almost from the ground itself, weightless for a moment.

"'How could you be so heavy?'" the priest quoted the saint.

"'You carried more across that water,' the child said. 'You carried the Christ Child, Himself, and all of his believers.' The saint did not believe, so the Child left a sign. 'Put your staff in the ground by your hut and see what has happened by dawn,' he said. Then the Child disappeared.

"The very next morning, a date palm bloomed where the staff had been planted: a true miracle."

"You, my son," Father Giovanni said, "are stronger in body and in faith than you know. Listen always for a soft knock on your door." The priest made the sign of the cross over Cristoforo's head, then turned on his heel, his robes swirling out against his ankles.

Back at the altar, he switched to speaking Latin again, and completed the Mass as if nothing special had happened.

After alms were collected for the poor, Cristoforo's mother dragged him toward the back of the cathedral. Along the side, they passed altars donated by the fishermen, the metalsmiths, and the stonemasons. Cristoforo opened the wooden gate at the weavers' guild altar and waited for his mother to enter. As they knelt together at the rail, Cristoforo tried to form a prayer, but his mind and legs still trembled. He had always known the Saint Cristoforo story. Until today, it had never meant so much.

Cristoforo refused to come home to eat afterward. He had to spend some time alone, thinking.

"Taking your coin to the market?" Mama asked. "How will you spend it? Honeyed figs? Sweet meats and raisins? A meal at the castle and a dance with the princess?"

Cristoforo smiled but shook his head, no. He waved good day to his mother and promised to be home by dark.

Cristoforo glanced at the path leading to the market square. That way lay sweets and jugglers, puppet shows and baubles—the stuff of children. Criminals hung from the gallows there beside the heretics and nonbelievers. They made for a grand display as they died, and were a fine warning for all. Dogs and pigs wandered free, and the rats fed under the tables at midday.

Cristoforo turned toward the waterfront instead. He sat dangling his feet over a dock and thought. This water led to Spain. To the land of red-haired people. And it led even beyond that. He closed his eyes and longed to feel the steady rocking of a large ship again.

"Ha!" Cristoforo's body stiffened as hands grabbed his shoulders from behind and pushed him toward the water. At the last second, he felt himself being pulled back from the edge.

"Never," the cabin boy said, and eased himself down beside Cristoforo. "Never would I think weaver's work was so hard. My hands are limp as seaweeds today—colored red from dyeing the yarn in the wool too. And what has happened to my skin?" He spread his fingers wide and stared at his palms. "Where are my calluses off to? I need them!"

Cristoforo laughed and spread his hands to show bloody patches.

"Ouch," the sailor said.

"Your hands were made soft by lanolin," Cristoforo explained. "Mine too. If not washed out with lye soap, lanolin makes wool sweaters smell sheepy—but it makes them waterproof, too."

"What does it *do* to your hands?" the cabin boy asked, sniffing at his red palms and wrinkling his nose.

"Lanolin makes a weaver's skin smooth and soft as a maiden's kiss."

"And I suppose you know from experience?" the sailor teased.

"Nay," Cristoforo admitted with a laugh. "I have stolen no kisses—yet."

"Nor have I," the cabin boy said. "Say, my name is Saul."

Cristoforo took a step backward. "'Saul'? Are you a Jew? A Moslem?" He was not sure he was supposed to be talking with a heathen.

"I am a sailor," Saul said firmly. "Now, give me your name."

"I am a Cristoforo." He paused, thinking of the priest's words. This sailor would be gone forever with the morning's tide. He could share a secret without worry. "I am a Cristoforo," he said, "who doesn't know how to sail, but must someday cross the waters."

Saul stared at him, then nodded slowly. "The sea calls to some of us." They locked glances, then stared out through the harbor. "A sailor must know knots," Saul said, breaking the silence. "I could teach you the ones you will need."

"You would share your craft outside your guild?" Cristoforo knew he was grinning like a simpkin.

"Aye," Saul said, nodding. "But first, I am hungry."

"Me too," Cristoforo said. "Let us wander to the market and spend this together." He pulled his saint's day coin from his pocket and jumped to his feet. "I'll race you to the sweets stall!"

CHAPTER THREE
MARCO POLO

A few years later, Papa's business was going well, so he could finally afford to send Cristoforo and Bartolo to a guild school. "The shop will be yours after I die," he said to his sons. "To carry it on, you will have to know the legal terms in contracts, and some figuring. A few weeks of school will give you what you need."

"Quiet, class," Master Oligo greeted the boys from the altar at the front of the classroom. Cristoforo stared around the great drafty masons' hall. Stone carving tools and measuring devices were chiseled into the walls. A church Bible lay open on the altar in the front. The masons started their meetings here with a religious ceremony, just as the weavers' guild did in their hall.

"Masons, sit here," Master Oligo said, and pointed. They got the front row of benches, of course. "Weavers on yon benches."

Cristoforo took his place, proud to represent his trade guild. Another weaver hissed at him. "You?" he whispered. "Your papa spent time in debtors' prison. The Colombo name has brought shame to the guild."

Cristoforo's face burned. That was not fair! And Bartolo did not need to hear it either. He felt his hands curl into fists.

"Besides," said another weaver's child, who slid into the row, "you might live inside the city gate now, but your family came from the hills. You will never be truly one of us."

Cristoforo slumped next to Bartolo on the bench. It was always like this—and always would be.

"The smiths," said Master Oligo, calling

boys to their benches. "The jewelers . . ."

As others shuffled into their places, Cristoforo busied himself by getting out his figures. Papa had said, "You have to know how to add and subtract so you will not be cheated by paying customers." Cristoforo did not care about selling cloth to housewives. He had decided to go to sea instead.

He had not told Papa about that decision. Papa's own father had been a master weaver. So had Mama's father, and her uncles, too. Weaving was the family business. He knew Papa would be angry about his choice, even after Father Giovanni's speech in church. Weaving was an honorable trade, but the sea was so exciting! Cristoforo stared out through the window.

"This class may interest even you, young Colombo," Master Oligo said as he settled into the chairman's seat at the head of the room. "Who has heard of the great Marco Polo?"

One of the mason's children raised his

hand. "He lived in the far Orient, did he not?"

"Aye. In the twelve hundreds," Master Oligo confirmed. "And how do we know of this now, two hundred years later?"

"My mama told me," Bartolo blurted. Cristoforo twisted around to glare as many others chuckled.

"Eyes forward, young men," the teacher snapped. "We know of Marco Polo and his adventures because they were written down. At first, monks copied his journals by hand. That took months for every single book. Only a few years ago, in Germany, a fellow invented something called a printing press. Now the volumes are being printed fast enough to make one dizzy—almost two books a day! Perhaps someday each of you might get to see a printed book."

"Are we going to learn to *read*?" a goldsmith asked, astonished.

The teacher laughed. "Of course not. Trades

people have no need of that. Besides, *The Book of Marco Polo* is in Latin." Colombo felt his shoulders sag. All those secrets locked away from him! "But," the teacher went on, "you could learn to read if you took up the cloth and became priests." Laughter scattered among the boys along with a few groans. Then the teacher said something that made Cristoforo sit up straight. "The cleverest among you could learn reading later in life."

Cristoforo nodded in promise to himself. He would learn to read, someday, and learn Latin, too. He had learned sailing knots. He was working in secret now with the navigators to learn how to read maps and plot a course. Of course, Bartolo had found out. He'd promised to not tell Papa so long as he got to learn too.

"'Tis a wonderment." Master Oligo's voice pulled Cristoforo back again. "Marco Polo did what no man has done before or since. His books tell us he sailed east with his father and an uncle to Constantinople. There, he joined a caravan, riding across vast deserts of Arabia on lumpy-backed animals like horses, called camels. Then he sailed east still farther across the Persian Sea."

"Was he there yet?" a cooper asked.

"Nay. Not even close. He still had to march across the great deserts of Gobi. It took three and a half years to reach Cathay [modern China] and the fabulous court of the Kublai Kahn in Peking." By now, every boy was leaning forward on his bench. The teacher's eyes got dreamy. "The kahn kept ten thousand servants—all dressed in silks and satins, jeweled with emeralds, diamonds, and pearls. He owned every gold and silver mine in the huge land. Even his palace roofs were gold. His zoos held every animal, from chittering monkeys and colorful parrots to the great-mouthed serpent beasts that swam in the water. His summer home had a hunting preserve stocked with deer and horses and elephants as big as an ocean ship."

"Marco Polo stayed there for seventeen years, did he not?" one of the mason's boys said, showing off. Master Oligo hurried on, explaining that Polo had been held captive, but had earned the Kahn's admiration and friendship. Finally Polo was allowed to travel with—and then *for*—the great kahn. He was entrusted to take a bride-to-be on the long voyage from Cathay to her husband in Persia [modern Iran]. For two years they sailed through the South China Sea, across the Indian Ocean, rounded India, sailed north on the Arabian Sea, and through the Strait of Hormuz.

Cristoforo realized that he was rocking on the bench in time to the exotic names. Embarrassed, he cleared his throat.

"Master Colombo seems to be bored," Master Oligo said harshly, "so I will finish quickly and get to the end of the story." All around Cristoforo, boys hissed.

"The groom had died, but Marco Polo delivered the bride, anyway, then sailed to Persia, through the Black Sea, and then through our dear ocean here and home to Venice." At the name of their hated rival city-state, the boys hissed all the louder. Master Oligo spread his hands for quiet. "Later, we caught the Venetian spying in our city. Polo was thrown in a Genovese jail." The guild teacher waited for the cheers to die down before he finished the story. "Polo told the stories in jail, and one fellow there could read. He could write, too. He wrote down Polo's tales, and although no one has been there for two hundred years," he finished with a flourish, "that is how we know the wonders of the East Indies."

A silence filled the guildhall as every boy saw himself in Polo's adventure. Finally, the church bells roused the class. "Blessed Saints!" Master Oligo sputtered. We have sums to do yet, and a few Latin words you'll need for legal dealings."

The afternoon wore on, but Cristoforo was not there. He was dreaming of meeting the Kublai Khan.

"Tell Papa that Master Oligo wanted me to stay after classes," Cristoforo told Bartolo. "I'm going out to catch sardines tonight."

"Take me!" Bartolo pleaded.

"Someone has to go home and pretend to Mama and Papa that I am on dry land, Barti," Cristoforo said. "With the money I make selling my catch, I will buy another lesson with the new chart maker in town."

"You will share?" Bartolo asked.

"Aye," Cristoforo answered. He pulled Barti's cap off and rubbed his hair. "I always share what I know with my first mate." Bartolo grabbed for his cap, but Cristoforo held it out of reach. "Promise a good story to cover my absence?" he demanded.

"I would rather tell the truth."

"Not yet, simpkin," Cristoforo told his brother. "'Tis a scene I would put off for another year." He pulled Bartolo's cap down over his eyes.

"Cris, you knave!" Bartolo's angry cry followed him down to the dock.

"You have nearly missed the tide," Antonio scolded.

"Oligo had more to say than an old woman," Cristoforo told his fishing partner. He tossed his scholar's cloak under the dock. "Is the net in the boat?"

"And the torches, too. It will be good and dark tonight, so the fish will all rush toward the light. But I will not be with you." Cristoforo froze. "'Twill be a calm night,"

Antonio reassured him. "Look yonder: the first stars in a clear sky. You know the ropes. We two have gone out often enough. You have grown strong at the oars and wise about the rocks. Stay close in to land, and you will do well."

Cristoforo crossed himself and got into a wooden rowboat. He sat down facing the back end of the boat. "Stern," he reminded himself, and gave a quick glance over his shoulder. The mouth of the harbor seemed farther away in the dusk, from a boat, alone. He took a deep breath, settled the oars into the oarlocks, and nodded to Antonio. His friend untied the bowline and threw it down into the boat.

Cristoforo dug the oars into the water and pulled away. The reassuring *slap-plop* of the swells against its hull made him feel brave. "Like Marco Polo setting off alone," he told himself, and pulled harder. He stared up toward the decks of the sailing vessels lying at anchor in the harbor. They floated wide and tall against the sunset, bristling with masts and spars and hung with a webbing of ropes. Cristoforo had watched them take on loads of grains and hides; great bulky cargoes. Now and then a sailor waved at him. More often, they stood silent, watching him crawl past, oar stroke by stroke.

As it grew darker, Cristoforo pretended he was working with a dozen other men, rowing a great galley ship, slender and shallow, full of spices and gems. Merchants from Venice used that kind of boat. He shook his head. Those unfaithful knaves still had dealings with the Moslem infidels of North Africa, Moorish Spain, and the Middle East. Venice had richer trade than ours, he thought. Their galleys might be faster. But Genoese ships had enough depth to hold bulky cargoes—or to sail where Marco Polo had gone.

Suddenly his boat lurched to the side as a grating sound ran along its hull. "Zounds!" Cristoforo swore. "The rocks!" He quickly paddled with one oar. The next swell lifted him up and raked his boat against the rocks again. Cristoforo peered into the darkness. The swells were bigger. The wind had picked up too. Cristoforo stood up. Where was he? At the top of the next swell, he caught a glimpse of city lights. Then the rowboat lurched again, and he fell to the seat.

He flailed in the darkness to find the oars. His hand smacked into one, then slammed against the other. "Row," he told himself sternly. How could he have gotten so far away from the shallows where the sardines schooled? And how was he going to get back in, against the wind and the tide?

He looked about the boat. It suddenly felt very small, with the blackness all around. And beneath him. He tried not to think of the sharks and monsters in the water, and the giant octopi lurking in the depths. He rowed harder, then looked over his shoulder.

He had turned completely around! How had that happened? He was rowing with both arms. Cristoforo thought quickly. He could barely feel the hand that he'd slammed into the wooden oar. Pain shot up one arm. Had he been pulling harder on the other side? He wanted to pray for strength, but couldn't spare a hand to cross himself.

Instead, he decided to row using only half-strength on his good side. That way, he hoped, he could head toward home and get there—eventually. He kicked at Antonio's net by his feet. Why had he ever thought he could manage a boat alone? He could not even open up the torch for his own comfort!

Cristoforo jumped when something tapped against his foot. He was not alone in the boat! His mind raced. *A sea monster? A spirit? A demon?* He kept rowing as hard as he could with his sore arm and half-strength with the other, but he pulled his feet up off the floor of the boat. "Who is there?" he called, staring into the inky darkness at the bottom of the boat.

Sparkles of light flickered around his feet! Cristoforo froze. The glitters twinkled back and forth, back and forth. It was the same rhythm as the waves. Cristoforo looked up. The sky was full of stars! He relaxed. Their light was reflected on the water in his boat. Some sailors could read the stars, he knew. For now, knowing there was starlight was enough.

And a moon was rising, peeking over the forts of the hills behind Genoa. Cristoforo rowed calmly for a few minutes. If something was in the boat with him, he would see it soon. He peered hard, concentrating. The boat was empty in the moonlight. He was alone. At this rate, it might take all night, but he knew exactly where home was. He was going to survive—and, if Bartolo had done his job, he would be home before his parents knew he was gone.

"Nay! Not so!" Cristoforo yelped aloud when the tapping against his foot began again. He stared down at the cork floats from the net. They bobbed in ankle-deep water. His boat was leaking! Cristoforo stopped rowing and felt along the wet boards where they had raked along the rocks. "Zounds!" he swore. There was a splintery dent where water sloshed in every time the swells hit the side.

Could he make it to the dock before the boat filled? He squinted his eyes and looked around. A huge, shadowy shape loomed off the left side of his boat. The port side, he thought. He sat down and began rowing again. This time he called out, "Ahoy!" with every seventh stroke.

At last, an answer floated down from the

deck far above. "Throw me a line," Cristoforo pleaded. "My boat is taking on water. I can't make it in, and I can't . . . can't swim." He hated the near sob in his voice.

A hearty laugh answered his plea, and the sharp slap of something hit the water near him. "A ladder, m'boy," the voice called, "and a line. Tie up thy boat and hold fast the ladder. We will haul thee up."

Cristoforo bit his lip against the pain in his hand as he was yanked upward. "Thank God for thee," he said, when he could finally speak on deck. A small knot of sailors pressed closely in the dark, looking him over, under a lantern.

"You are a poor seaman," the ship's captain declared.

"I am but a weaver's apprentice," Cristoforo admitted. "I am learning, though. I long for the sea."

"The sea almost got you, matey!" a sailor laughed.

"My name, 'Cristoforo,' draws me to the water," Cristoforo said. "I feel I have no choice." In the lantern light, he saw the men cross themselves.

"Then you bring the blessings of the saint to this voyage," the captain said. "We will be docking tomorrow at first light. Can you wait until the morn to see your master, young weaver? For tonight, we will be proud to carry you and your luck."

Cristoforo looked out over the rail at the moon river stretching bright across the water. These sailors welcomed him, unlike his own guild brothers. Aboard ship, his name meant something good. "It is my honor," he said.

CHAPTER FOUR

TO SEA!

"You utter simpkin!" Papa roared. "Alone in a boat? At night? 'Tis worse than foolhardy!"

"I have fished at night before," Cristoforo said, rubbing his sore hand. "I sell my catch and pay the chart maker for lessons."

"What?" Mama's voice was shrill. "Is the weaver's trade not fine enough for the likes of you?" The new baby girl in her arms started crying. "Hush, Bianchetta, hush."

"*This* is your craft, son." Papa spread his arms wide, pointing to fine woolen fabrics lying folded on shelves and baled for market. "We feed and shelter you as we do any apprentice to our trade. You owe us more than sardines."

"I give you fair labor in the day," Cristoforo said. "So does Bartolo."

"Barti?" Mama said. "What has my Barti to do with this?" Her legs seemed to give way, and she sat on the bale of fabric. Cristoforo looked at his brother and shrugged.

"Cris is an explorer just like Marco Polo," Bartolo said, moving to stand next to his brother. "I will sail with him someday."

Cristoforo felt his face flush hot. *An explorer.* Even he had not thought of his future that way. He put his hand on Bartolo's shoulder.

"Then you will both die." Papa said. "Sea storms or monsters, pirates or Moorish thieves, you will perish at sea. Who will care for us and our shop?"

"Cris," Mama begged over the baby's head, "I long to see the masterpiece your clever fingers can create. You could be a wise master weaver. I dream of the day you chair the weavers' guild of Genoa." Cristoforo began shaking his head. Didn't his mother know how the other weavers felt about the Colombo family? Nobody here would ever be elected to guild office. But Mama went on hoping. "Someday, Cris, you might even be elected alderman for the city —"

"Quiet, woman," Papa said. "Can you not see? Cris is but a child. He will come back to the fold. Bartolo, too." He stroked his beard. "Mayhap a few voyages will cure their lust."

Cristoforo stood tall. "What do you mean?" he asked. "Do I have your leave to go to sea?"

"Nay. You owe me four more years on your apprenticeship. You will stay and learn with me. But you should know the markets for our goods. You may sail with the next shipment to Corsica."

"Nay, oh, nay," Mama wailed, and the baby

cried along. "Do not send him. What if the ship sinks?"

"Boats shuttle back and forth to the island of Corsica every day, woman," Papa said. "We do a fair trade along the coast, too, where the sailor never loses sight of the shore. Once Cristoforo has had his fill of seasickness, he will come home to the safety of hearth and loom."

Cristoforo wanted to hug his papa. Instead, he turned and grabbed Bartolo's cap. "Race you to the docks!" he said, and tore out of the house.

A merchant ship was due to set sail within days. The captain was willing to take Cristoforo for a percentage of the sales the boy made in the ports.

At first, Cristoforo was not welcome. "Out of the way!" "Get below." "Watch your head!"

The sailors had little time for their red-haired passenger—until they learned he was hungry to learn seamanship.

"This turns the rudder," the mate said, pushing on the long wooden tiller. "Hold it there. Can you feel the water pushing back?"

"One hand for yourself, one hand for the ship," a sailor said, laughing, as he helped Cristoforo up off the deck. "Keep one hand free to grab hold if you need to. You'll get your sea legs."

"See yon cliff? Here it is on the chart," the navigator said. "If we sail northwest by west, we should end up where?" He waited while Cristoforo plotted a course. "Nay, lad. Check the chart's compass rose if you have forgotten your directions. Now, try again."

Sailors did not get many second chances. Punishments were swift and brutal. That made sense to Cristoforo. Disobeying orders might mean the deaths of many of the deckhands. Next to death, a whipping meant little, he thought. Except to the disobedient sailor, bleeding, bruised, and expected to get back to work with the next watch.

"Foul weather coming," the captain said to Cristoforo one morning as they stared at a colorful sunrise. When Cristoforo asked how he knew, the captain explained, "Red sky at night, sailor's delight. Red sky in the morning, sailors take warning. God gave us that saying, right in the Bible." They both crossed themselves. "There are rules like that aplenty, and ways to read the winds, too. I'll show you."

A strong, tall boy like Cristoforo was often a help. He began to hear: "Give me a hand here, lad." "Hold this down." "Grab the line with us and heave!" Soon, it was: "Cris can do it." "Call Cris!"

When the sailmaker found that Cristoforo could work with a needle, he put him to work mending a sail. "Stitching comes in handy after a battle, too," he said. "Sometimes the sailmaker doubles as a ship's surgeon, sewing seams in skin as tidy as in canvas." Cristoforo's skill with knots was welcomed everywhere, and the navigator let him make chart maker's notes to correct the charts. They were astonished to find that a weaver's son even knew how to swab a deck.

"We call this rope a 'halyard,'" a deckhand said. "Halyards raise or lower the sails." There were so many new words to learn! But Cristoforo seemed to have a real skill in learning new languages. He soon knew that "reefing" a sail meant tying it down so it caught less wind. Each sail had its own name. A "mainsail" was on the main mast. A "top-sail" hung above that. "Going about" meant turning. Cristoforo's mind was dizzy with new facts when he finally lay down belowdecks to sleep. His stomach did not get dizzy, though, even up on the watchtower above the mainsail.

"Did you suffer seasickness as Papa said?" Bartolo asked on the dock when the ship finally pulled in.

"Nay," Cristoforo answered truthfully, "but now the land seems to be riding the swells." They both laughed as he staggered down the path toward home.

Domenico approved of his reports of sales. The merchants had asked Cristoforo for more shipments and special colors. "It is good to have an agent abroad doing business," he said, "but only now and then. For now, get back to the looming room. Your mother needs help instructing a new apprentice."

"Well come, Cris," Mama said with a hug.

She swiped a tear aside and told him, "Barti has tried to teach this little simpkin. He still cannot tie the long warp yarns onto the loom. You try."

Cristoforo grinned. "Look closely," he told the young boy. But when Cristoforo tried to finger the fine-spun wool, it caught on his rough skin. Hauling on the harsh ropes had left his hands covered with tiny cuts, scratches, and calluses. The feathery yarn stuck to spots of tar and pitch that dotted his skin too. He felt as clumsy as the young apprentice did as he tried to tie the simplest knots of the weaver's trade.

"Never mind," Mama finally said, and sighed deeply. "I suppose I will have to do it myself. "Go card out some of the new fleeces in the shed. 'Twill be good for your useless sailor's hands."

Cristoforo was glad to escape to the quiet of

the fleece shack. He breathed its familiar scent and sneezed at the dust. Somehow, this did not smell like home anymore. After the clean sea breezes, this just smelled foul. Cristoforo chose one of the spiny seed pods from a small pile of teasels on the dirt floor. He dragged a three-legged stool to a sunny spot in the doorway. Sighing, he opened a great bag of fleece and sank his fingers in to grab a handful.

Cristoforo sat down and began using the stiff spines on the teasel to comb out the tangled wool. He only glanced once at the work ahead of him. It all had to be ready to spin into tight threads or fluffy yarns. He daydreamed about the boat and the sailors. He imagined being an explorer. Sometimes he sang as he pulled the long fibers free. "A penny for a spool of thread, a penny for a teasel, that's the way the money goes . . ." He remembered squealing with surprise when the marker, the "weasel," popped up on Mama's spinning wheel when the run of yarn had been spun. Of course, he was younger then. . . . Bits of leaves and sheep droppings, dirt, and dander sifted to the ground between his knees. When the dense gray tangle had been carded to a puff of satiny white hair, he set it aside to be spun into yarn and took out another greasy handful.

The doorway darkened once. "How was it, Cris, in truth?" asked Bartolo, who stood silhouetted against the sun.

"Twas better than anything we dreamed, Barti," Cristoforo said. "We both need to study more often with the town's mapmaker. Navigators show the way onboard ship. The chart makers show the new paths to others. Therein lies the glory of exploring."

"You want glory, Cris?" Bartolo asked.

"I think everyone yearns for fame and

fortune," Cristoforo told his brother.

"Not as much as you do," Bartolo said. He watched the teasel fly in Cristoforo's sweaty hands. "You do not look so famous now," he teased.

Cristoforo lurched at him, and then calmly pulled the fleece between two teasels again a few times. "There's not much more we can do on dry land to prepare—but swim. We must both learn to swim for our lives. All else is experience." He looked at his hands. They were already healing from the lanolin.

"Can I have the next turn sailing on a merchant ship?" Bartolo asked, his voice plaintive.

Cristoforo smiled. "I will tell Papa that the more often we go sailing, the quicker we will tire of it. He will send us out often."

Bartolo grinned.

★　★　★　★

Cristoforo Colombo's hands went from rough to smooth and back again over the next years as he learned two trades. The harsh, rowdy life of a sailor called to him. So did the mysteries of the sea. He had no interest in his father's precious guild and its formal meetings in the weavers' hall. Everything about sheep and weaving was well known. There was always adventure on the sea.

The Moslem forces had grown powerful, raiding merchant vessels and seizing them and their cargoes. Their galleys lurked in coves and sailed in convoys, sometimes even attacking peaceful towns ashore. After raising the crescent flag over the ancient Christian city of Constantinople, they were getting bolder, trying to control trade routes throughout the Mediterranean. The Moors held North Africa and Córdoba on the southern edge of Spain, too. They could sail from many ports.

Cristoforo had seen their ships, and hundreds of others. He had sailed on many voyages, once traveling on a three-masted ship as far east as Chios Island [off modern Turkey]. This trip crossed the open Mediterranean Sea instead of hugging the shoreline for safety. Cristoforo knew now how wide the ocean could feel and how much smaller Genoa was than other cities. He had many skills as seaman and navigator.

None of this mattered to his father. The two men fought again and again in those years. Finally, at eighteen, Cristoforo completed his apprenticeship. His father had to face the truth: His firstborn son was leaving the weaving trade. Bartolo had left a year earlier, journeying to Lisbon to become a chart maker. Bartolo was only a second son. He would not inherit the business. Bianchetta was a girl, so she would not inherit it either.

"At least we have another heir now," Papa

grumbled, patting the head of his new little son, Diego. "Go now, Cristoforo. Abandon us if you will. Never think to poison Diego's mind with your adventurer's dreams."

Beginning when Christopher Columbus was twenty, the historical record of his life is more complete. We know something of his whereabouts and his actions, including his first great seafaring adventure in 1476. . . .

★   ★   ★

CHAPTER FIVE

MAN OVERBOARD!

As wind began to fill the sails, twenty-five-year-old Cristoforo glanced back only once at his family in Genoa. "Fare thee well." He could not hear his mama saying it, but he knew she would call "Farewell!" until her voice went hoarse. Bianchetta stood to one side, and little Diego held his mama's hand. Cristoforo did not waste time looking for his father at the dock.

Domenico Colombo had goods aboard one of the ships, but this time, Cristoforo was not sailing as a merchant. Now he was just a common seaman in a special, armed fleet. Genoese craftsmen of many guilds had contributed to this desperate venture. Many of the city's smaller ships had been lost in raids by enemy countries or to pirates. This time, five ships planned to sail east and on out of the Mediterranean. That way they could avoid ambushes near shore. They would run out through the narrow Straits of Gibraltar and onto the endless Ocean Sea [the modern Atlantic Ocean]. From there, they would head to Portugal, England, and Flanders to sell their wares.

All five boats were galleys, sleek and swift. Each had long oars for power in case the wind failed at a dangerous time. Their cargo holds were stuffed with the best Genoa had to offer: fabrics and jewelry, olive oil and wines, cheese and more. These merchant ships also carried extra guns and small-bore cannons.

"Heave!" the first mate called. "Heave!" Cristoforo pulled on the halyard along with the others. "Heave." All bent to the task of raising the mainsail and its heavy wooden spar up the main mast. Finally, Cristoforo heard, "Tie her off!" He faltered, trying to loop the rope, thick as a man's wrist, around the heavy wooden belaying pin.

"You will have to be quicker'n that or you will feel the lick o'the cat," the sailor beside him muttered. Cristoforo shuddered. He'd seen what a cat-o'-nine-tails did to skin. A normal whip left welts and often drew blood, but each of the metal tips on the cat's many "tails" was designed to cut and cut deep. Cristoforo shuddered again and promised himself to move quicker.

"Over here!" the first mate yelled, and Cristoforo ran to obey. There was no watching the navigator on this trip; no picking up information here and there. In the first weeks, Cristoforo learned to jump to attention and heave past exhaustion. The rippling sound of wind in the vast sails overhead went on, day and night. When the wind slacked off, drums beat time to help the sailors rowing in the galley below the deck.

Every day was divided into four watches. Life was timed by an hourglass. It took an hour for sand to sift down from this top compartment into the bottom of the glass. Then a cabin boy turned the hourglass over to start it again. The timing of the watches was so important that there were extra hourglasses aboard in case one broke.

Bells also rang to call the sailors to daily church services on deck too. For the first week there was little Cristoforo could do during his off-watch but curl up in the hold and sleep. Little by little, his body adapted until finally he had the energy to stay awake and talk with the other seamen. He also began to notice the stink of the hold.

It wasn't a sewage smell belowdecks, exactly. Sailors sat in special seats or rope slings out at the head of the boat to drop their body waste into the water. The hold was full of the stink of stagnant water from the puddles below. Some water always collected in the bilge at the bottoms of boats. Bilge water sloshed quietly in time with the waves outside and stank of rotting litter inside.

The sleeping area belowdecks was filled with the smell of unwashed bodies, too. When there was rough weather, sailors often got seasick in the hold. When the cook's food was worse than usual, the hold filled with a sour gassy smell. Cristoforo smiled once, thinking that all this stench made the smell of dirty sheep's wool seem sweet as Mama's rose water.

In their private time, most of the sailors talked of women, swearing and bragging and using rude speech. That was not Cristoforo's style. He spent more time with those who preferred devotions to dirty stories. They had traveled far and had much to share. Often the talk went to finding a new trade route to the Orient. "Old Prince Henry the Navigator, bless his soul, he almost made it," a grizzled old man said from a corner of the hold one night.

"I think he was right, trying to sail down around Africa." This came from a dark-skinned man with one eye. "Didn't get past the equator, though. That's no surprise. I've heard tell the seas boil with the heat down there."

"Even if Henry the Navigator didn't make it in his lifetime," another said, spitting on the planking, "I do believe others will find a way for sure—and soon."

"A new route to the Far East [modern India, China, Japan]?" Cristoforo sat up and knocked his head against the low ceiling. "Not the way Marco Polo went? We could stop battling the Moors! We could make a fortune trading spices and fine fabrics!" He rubbed his head. "Who is looking for this new way?"

"The Portuguese throne gives the boldest sea captains in Lisbon money now and anon," the gray-haired sailor said, scratching at his head. "I hate lice," he said. Pulling one of the tiny biting insects from his hair, he popped it. "These explorers keep trying to swing up around Africa to meet the Kublai Kahn in Cathay. Or mayhap they'll sail on to Cipango [modern Japan], where the Fuji Mountain stands capped with snow."

"The kahn died long ago," Cristoforo told them.

"Well, the explorer who finds the route will be rich and famous."

"If he could carry the word of Christ with him, even better," Cristoforo said, a plan growing in his head. "He could convert the infidels and heathens."

"There already was a Saint Cristoforo, young 'un," the old man said. "That job is filled." They all laughed.

"Feel that?" someone said. There was a silence in the dark hold. "The seas are running longer. It is nothing like the great Ocean Sea swells, but we will be there soon."

Cristoforo moved to go up on deck and look over the rail at the water.

"The watch will be over soon enough, lad," the old sailor said. "Best we sleep now."

They curled up on the floor or settled onto trunks and bales. Soon there was no sound below but snoring and the scurry of rat's paws.

"Look lively. First mate's coming," the one-eyed man warned Cristoforo. They had sailed a few days past Gibraltar. "But peek at that coastline. You see the cliff up ahead?" Cristoforo glanced shoreward and nodded, though he kept splicing the rope as he'd been told. "Yon land is Portugal."

Cristoforo stared. "My brother is rumored to be at work there."

"The rope, simpkin!" the old man hissed. Cristoforo bent to his task as the first mate strode past. "Now," Cristoforo's friend went on, "we watch for Cape Saint Vincent. There will be an 'all hands' call there, mark my words."

"Why?" Cristoforo asked.

"All Christian ships dip their sails in respect to the saint as they pass," the one-eyed man said. We should see it as soon as we clear Sagres point, yonder."

Cristoforo glanced up at the rocky headland jutting into the sea. A flash of white caught his eye, and he looked again. Then he leaped to his feet. "Ships ahoy!" he yelled.

"Ships ahoy!" echoed from the watch platform up on the main mast. All eyes were watching Sagres point now. Two galleys under full sail and rowing double time streaked out from behind the cliffs. Another followed.

"Look to their colors! They're French," a sailor said, dancing. "There be a battle ahead for sure!"

The ship's bell began ringing wildly. "All men to stations!" the captain's voice cracked with excitement. "All men to battle stations!"

The deck was full of rushing bodies, but the ships could only glide toward each other. When the men stood ready, there was time left to watch—and worry. "There be eight of their ships," one sailor moaned, "and only five of ours!"

The fleets closed in on one another, maneuvering only as the winds allowed. Soon the plan of attack became clear. "That near ship aims to ram us straight on!" someone yelled. Cristoforo looked over the rail at the water far below and swallowed. He said a quick prayer and crossed himself.

"Ready!" the captain's voice cut through the clamor. "Take aim. On my count now . . ." *Fight off the grappling hooks,* Cristoforo reminded himself. He had a job. He pulled his knife from its sheath as he pushed through the confusion to the railing.

The French vessel was hurtling toward them now. He could see the French sailors' faces; their eyes. Cristoforo thought they did not look all that different. Not evil, certainly. He had not expected that. "Fire!"

At the captain's command, a volley of shots rang out, some from the Genoese boat, many more from the French. A cannonball slammed into a Frenchman before Cristoforo's eyes. Splinters flew from the ship's rail under Cristoforo's hands. They were shooting at *him*!

Closer the French boat came and closer still. At the last minute, they swerved. Their sails swung and snapped taut. The French boat lay side by side with the merchantman now. They'd reloaded their cannons, and the balls slammed across the deck in a cloud of gunpowder smoke. One hit the Genoese main mast, and it splintered as easily as a railing.

"Timber!" someone called. Cristoforo looked up to see the sail and hundreds of feet of heavy rope snaking downward at him. He screamed and dodged. "Steady!" the one-eyed sailor said beside him. His face was bloody. "Now they grapple."

A Frenchman stood on the rail of his ship, twirling a huge hook on a thick chain. A bullet struck him down. The next sailor managed to send his hook over the merchantman's rail near Cristoforo. It dug into the wood and scraped a long trough across the deck. Cristoforo grabbed it with both hands and fought to haul it free, but the point was anchored in the wood. One Frenchman leaped aboard, then another.

Cristoforo raised his knife, but a blow to his head knocked him sideways. He staggered to the side, then tripped over the torn mainsail. A fist found his face, then he was falling. He tumbled head over heels, slamming against the ship's hull before he crashed. Cristoforo tried to scream, but water filled his mouth—salty water.

He flailed his arms and pulled himself to

the surface. A body dropped on him, then another. Cristoforo choked and swam desperately. He had to get clear of the narrow space between the hulls. Overhead, volleys of gunfire thundered and an explosion roared. Bits of planking and oars rained down, and the air thickened with smoke. *Swim,* Cristoforo told himself. *Swim for your life!*

A great wave broke over his head. Tossed under, he struggled up for air once again. At last, he made it clear of the ships and grabbed one of the oars floating nearby. He rested, panting, trying to make sense of the fiery scene. His ship's masts hung broken. Her smoking hull listed far to the side.

The French ship tightened its sails and pulled away, guns still blazing. Between the cannon fire, Cristoforo could hear men screaming. Suddenly his ship tilted up in the bow. She was going down! Cristoforo clawed through the water. The boat would suck him under as she sank. When a wave lifted him up, he saw the land. *Safety*, he thought. It was miles and miles away—much too far to swim. He paused to pray, then began stroking toward the shore.

CHAPTER SIX
EXPLORER

Cristoforo staggered onto the sand hours later. He finally let go of the oar. His wobbly legs let go too. "A miracle," he whispered. He sank to the ground with a prayer of thanks and slept.

He awoke to a rough shake of his shoulder. A man's voice was saying something in a foreign language. Cristoforo's groggy brain struggled to make sense of it. Over the crashing of waves on the beach, the man's strange words sounded familiar. He was speaking Portuguese! Cristoforo tried to answer with the few Portuguese words he had learned from shipmates. The man laughed loud and long. Cristoforo wondered what he had said and felt his face go red.

"My name, sir"—he propped himself up on one elbow, gave a friendly smile, and pressed his hand against his chest—"my name is Cristoforo Colombo." He hoped the man understood Genoese Italian.

"Ah," the man said with a big smile. "Italian." He pointed to the land behind him. "Here, you Cristovão Colom." He thumped Cristoforo on the chest and offered his hand.

"Nay," Cristoforo said, but the man had repeated this new name. "I must get to Lisbon," Cristoforo tried. He spoke in Italian, but very slowly and clearly. "Your capital city. Do you know a Bartolo"—he paused—"Bartolomo Colom, in Lisbon?"

"You come, Cristovão," the man said in Portuguese.

Cristoforo took the man's hand at last. "Cristovão," he repeated. A new name for a new place, he thought. It might come in handy to fit in with these Portuguese. And it looked like he would be here for a while. Cristovão glanced out at the smoking debris of his ship.

Now the fisherman made the motion of eating something. He put his arm out to help as Cristovão limped up the beach. He saw other seamen and French sailors lying on the sand. Fishermen were helping a few. Others were struggling to sit up on their own. Some lay still.

The fisherman's wife had dry clothes and a hot meal waiting for the survivors. The village folk had all seen the battle. They nursed the sailors who had made it to their beach. The wives and children welcomed the foreigners, and taught them enough Portuguese to get along. Days later, Cristovão sat in the sunshine with two or three other survivors from Genoa.

"We must go to Lisbon," he told them. He said he had no money, but that his brother was there. He explained that his brother was working as a chart maker.

"In Lisbon?" one of the men said wonderingly. "That is where all of the explorers' ships dock. That is where the news of new discoveries reaches land first!"

"There is need there for people who can change the old charts," Cristovão said. "I have learned that skill." The other men were ready to sail out with the next boat. Cristovão's plans were not so simple. He stared out over the ocean, thinking. He would go to Lisbon and learn. First, he would need to know more of the language, of course. And he would need to work with Bartolo for a while. But *Lisbon* . . . He smiled.

Lisbon was the center of the sailing world. There, Prince Henry the Navigator had gathered all the best astronomers and navigators, ship designers and builders—no matter what their race or religion. The ancient knowledge of the Arabs and the Africans, Romans and local fishermen was there for the taking.

Cristovão dreamed on. He would learn to read there. He might even take up writing—and speaking Latin, too! He would meet important people. And he would go to sea. To the land of the red-haired people, and perhaps beyond. . . .

"Cristoforo?"

"Ahoy, there, Colombo!" Cristovão blinked, and the Genovese men sitting around him laughed.

"Did you swallow that much salt water?" one of them guessed.

"Did you see that smile?" another teased. "Our Cris was swimming with a mermaid."

Cristovão shook his head. "We are in Portugal," he said firmly. "My name is Cristovão Colom, here." He stood up and stretched. "It is time we went to church." To their startled stares he answered, "We are here by a miracle. I will not waste this second chance at life."

★　★　★　★

"Welcome, Cris," Bartolomo said, giving his brother a fierce hug. "I thought you were dead! I heard that three of our ships went down. They sank seven long miles from the nearest land. I feared the worst." He wiped tears from his eyes, then laughed, then threw his arms about his older brother again.

"You've done well for yourself," Cristovão said, looking around the chart maker's tiny shop. Quill pens and rulers, ink bottles, and reference books lay around the edges of a wide drafting board. In the center, a ship's map of Africa lay open. "How old are you, Barti? Eighteen?"

Bartolomo laughed. "Eighteen and very lucky at cards, Cris. I won some money, then met the old chart maker. He had no sons and his vision was failing, so he sold me the business for a song."

Barti closed his map shop for the day. The brothers strolled to a tavern and talked until late. Cristovão told his brother of all his plans.

"Go to the docks, first," Bartolomo advised. "The other ships of your fleet are there being repaired, and others are hiring. You will be more help to me once you have earned enough money to survive. You need enough Portuguese to speak to customers."

"The ships are sailing out? Into the Ocean Sea?" Cristovão drained his flagon of ale and looked out the tavern window. "Which way are the docks?"

Cristovão signed onto another ship. He could have sailed south to the coast of Africa on a Portuguese ship for slaves and gold. He could have manned a smaller ship, making stops at local ports. He could have joined a navy, too. His decision was easy. He signed on with a Genoese merchantman heading to the far north. Here was a chance to make money, learn languages, and see the world.

At first, they skimmed the shore. Here and there were little cottages and a village or two. These did not matter to a sailor. The ships watched for marks on the land that would never change, like cliffs or mountains, the mouths of rivers or rocky ledges. These were marked on the charts that every boat carried. They were the kind of landmarks that Cristovão had made on charts back in Genoa as a teenager.

Soon, Cristovão's boat steered away from the shore of Portugal. They could not see land. With no landmarks to follow, the helmsman used dead reckoning to find the way. That meant he kept careful records of the direction sailed, the speed the ship had gone, the direction and strength of winds. He even included how far the wind might have blown the ship sideways in the water. Every day, he entered these records and plotted them right on the chart. That gave the helmsman a good idea of where the ship was. The next day's progress was measured from the last's.

Cristovão had seen this done on his voyage east from Genoa. That was on the Mediterranean, though. It was a sea ringed with land. If they got lost, sooner or later they would hit land and know where they were.

Here on the Ocean Sea it was different. Many thought the seawater boiled at the equator. True, explorers had gone that far south and survived. Few were willing to take the risk. Too far north and the seas turned to ice. Too far west and no one knew what would happen. The earth was round, of course. Everyone knew that. The vast open ocean might be full of monsters and horrors no one had even dreamed of. It had long been called the green sea of darkness.

True, a few small islands had been discovered out there. The Canary Islands lay to the south, off Africa. They were under Spanish rule. North of them, the Portuguese Madeira Islands grew grapes that made fine wines. More Portuguese-claimed islands lay farther out into the Ocean Sea and north. These were the Azores and the Cape Verde Islands. Beyond that, no land had ever been found—just endless, empty seas.

On this voyage, the helmsman kept Cristovão's course northward, toward known ports. During the sailing hours, Cristovão learned all he could about open ocean sailing. During his days on land he compared clothing and fabrics of local weavers. He attended church, of course. He tried to talk with the local sailors, too, to hear what they knew of the seas near their ports. He found people who could translate for him, and he forced himself to learn as much as he could of local languages.

Cristovão's ship stopped in Bristol, England, dropping off and taking on goods. It then sailed to Thule [modern Iceland]. The locals spun myths for him of Norse voyages to far, cold lands. Were these just stories, or had the Vikings really made other discoveries? Cristovão could not speak the language well enough to know for sure. The idea burned in his mind as he left for Galway, Ireland.

Here, as in England, many fair-skinned people lived. Many of them had hair as red as Cristovão's. He found something else more interesting. A couple of little boats had washed up on shore. Inside were people who had died of hunger or exposure. It was their faces that excited Cristovão. They looked just like people from paintings he had seen of Orientals. Were they from Cathay? How had they gotten to Ireland?

Cristovão's long voyage back to Lisbon gave him plenty of time to think about what he had seen. The Ocean Sea was wide and seemed endless. From a ship's deck you could see the curve of it at the horizon. It must wrap all the way around the globe. That meant there was a sea route that way to the Orient. Cristovão began to dream of discovering the trade route himself.

He was paid when he arrived back in Lisbon. Now he could invest in his brother's map shop. He had learned to speak fluent Portuguese. He began making money correcting old seafaring charts and creating new ones. Cristovão bought himself a copy of *The Book of Marco Polo* from one of the many new printers in Lisbon. He taught himself to read it. Since it was only a printed copy and not a precious hand-lettered edition, Columbus underlined words right in the book. Soon he began copying words and sentences in the wide margins, too. That way, he learned to write. He bought more books: a Bible, a natural history, and books on navigation, and history, too. All of their margins ended up full of his notes and thoughts. He carried these books with him on every trip.

Cristovão was finally getting an education. He was earning money, too. But he was no closer to getting his own ship. He had to find a way to meet the royalty of Portugal so he could apply for funding.

At a local chapel, a young woman caught his eye at Mass one day. "I am pleased to meet you, Cristovão Colom," she said, looking up at him. "You are the tallest man in Portugal—and you have the reddest hair and face, too!" Cristovão felt himself blush and he felt like a simpkin. "I am Doña Felipa Perestrello e Moniz. I live at the convent boarding school." A nun from the boarding school hurried her away before she could say more.

When he asked Bartolo about her, he learned that Doña Felipa came from an old noble family. "You have no hope with a girl like that," he scolded. "You are a nobody here. Her father was the first governor of one of the Madeira Islands. She is the granddaughter of one of Prince Henry the Navigator's best friends, too!"

Cristovão kept going to Mass at the chapel. The girl was attractive. She was interested in him. She might be his contact to high society. Little by little, in stolen conversations, a friendship began. Perhaps his exotic looks and Italian accent attracted her. Perhaps it was his worldly experience and his bold dream. This man intended to sail west across the Ocean Sea to the Orient! A romance bloomed under the nun's watchful eye. Later, Doña Felipa's widowed mother met the couple. She, too, approved.

Cristovão was twenty-eight when he married Felipa in 1479. Within a year, they moved from Lisbon to Porto Santo, the Madeiran Island far out in the Ocean Sea. There they had a son and named him Diego. Cristovão learned from all of the ships' pilots and captains who sailed in and out of the busy seaport. He learned, too, from his wife's family's papers—

charts and writings of the sea. During these years, he sailed to the African coast and back several times. He became an expert in navigation and learned how to bargain with foreign people. He also learned how the slave trade worked.

Cristovão knew he was ready. He wrote up his idea to sail west to the Orient. In order to appeal to an enterprising sponsor who would take a great risk—and expect great riches in return—Cristovão's proposal had to be presented as a clear business.

The plan had to spell out where Cristovão was going, too. People wanted to trade with both the West Indies [modern Afghanistan, India, Pakistan, and Iran] and the East Indies [modern Japan, China, Korea, Thailand, Vietnam, etc.]. Nobody was sure of the geography on the other side of the world. Cristovão lumped them all together as "the Indies." That way, he would succeed wherever he landed.

He titled his proposal "The Enterprise of the Indies" and made a fancy copy of it on parchment. All that was left was to find someone to finance his "Enterprise."

CHAPTER SEVEN
GRAND IDEA

Everything had fallen into place. Cristovão had the skills and knowledge to sail the known seas. He had contacts now among ship captains and the rich ruling class. He had gone over and over his figures. He was convinced that the earth was smaller than many people thought. That meant that sailing west to Cathay was very possible. His "Enterprise of the Indies" was ready to submit to the king of Portugal.

Cristovão could make a good case for his dream, too. Any country who found the trade route could claim it and make a fortune. The Catholic Church could save thousands of heathen souls. That would bring glory to the country and the pope's blessings. The Church would be getting the donations from all those new church members. And Cristovão? He figured he should get some of the profits of the income. It meant more than just money to him, though. Carrying the spirit of Christ across the water was his holy destiny.

Cristovão presented his case to the young King John II of Portugal. It seemed the right time. King John had financed many voyages of discovery. He had explorers and navigators on his payroll. One of his ships was just home from a trip to Africa. It had sailed up the Congo River and captured some Congolese natives. These black captives were in Lisbon, being turned into good Christians.

"Send me to the West," Cristovão argued. "My route is shorter than sailing all around Africa—if that is possible at all." King John seemed interested, so Cristovão talked and talked. He made his plan sound easy by claiming the distances were probably even smaller than he had figured. He raved about the riches, the gold and spices, the souls and glory. Cristovão's enthusiasm excited the king, until he called in his experts. In private, they told the king that this Genovese chart maker's figures were all wrong. Anyway, why should the Portugese ruler pay a stranger like Cristovão to do what his own sailors could do?

Cristovão got the king's final decision from a servant: "The king has no interest in your 'Enterprise.'"

It was a crushing blow.

Worse was to come. Cristovão's wife, Doña Felipa, got sick and died. Besides being a loving spouse, she had been a source of support and contacts for Cristovão. Now he and five-year-old Diego were alone.

Cristovão was not willing to give up his dream. He still needed to find a sponsor, someone who would finance the expedition. If not King John, who? He talked it over with his brother. Queen Isabella and King Ferdinand were rich enough. By combining her land and his, they had united a huge country, Spain. True, they were still fighting the Moors who held Granada in the south of their country. There was another reason that they might want to help "The Enterprise." For their faithfulness and their success in uniting Spain as a Christian country, Pope Alexander VI had named them official Catholic monarchs. New converts in the Orient would mean even more to the Spanish royalty than to King John II. Cristovão's confidence flooded back. There was hope for his dream in Spain.

Bartolo agreed to keep the chart-making business running in Lisbon. He would not care for Diego, though. He would not help pay any debts, either. Cristovão had lost a lot of money on a sugar shipment he had sailed to Madeira. It had also cost a great deal to live near the

Portuguese court and to dress like a successful explorer. He had nothing left but debt. The people he owed money to were getting impatient. Even if his marriage to Doña Felipe had made him part of the nobility by marriage, he still could be put in jail for not paying his debts.

To escape prison in 1485, Cristovão fled to Spain with Diego. They got off the boat in Palos. Within sight of shore, a great white building rose into the sky. "That is La Rábida," a dockhand told him in Spanish. "The Franciscans run the monastery there."

Cristovão hugged Diego. "We will go there," he told his hungry little boy. "The good monks will feed us."

Cristovão knocked on the heavy wooden door of the monastery. The man who answered was wearing a long brown cloak belted with a simple rope. "Well come, stranger. I am

Antonio de Marchena," he said. He told Cristovão that in Spain his name would be Cristóbal Colón. "If you wish success here, you must drop your Portugese name at once." The monastery offered him food and a safe home. Over supper, Antonio heard about Cristóbal's dream. The monk's eyes danced. He offered to enroll Diego at the monastery boys' school.

"I, myself, have studied astronomy and the place of the earth in God's universe." Antonio went on. "I have a friend who might be interested in financing your venture. Stay here a few days while I arrange a meeting for you."

In the meantime, Cristóbal struggled to learn Spanish. Many of the words were similar to Portuguese. The Spanish clothing styles were almost the same. The buildings, however, were different. Most of the land had been ruled by the Moors in the past, and the architecture was far fancier. When the Christians took over, they adorned the Moorish buildings with crosses and crucifixes to announce the new state religion.

Spain's Catholic monarchs ruled strictly. They insisted that everything—and everyone—agree with their beliefs. This came naturally to Cristóbal. He had grown up in the Catholic Church and had never questioned any of its teachings.

Others were not so lucky. Nonbelievers were tortured publicly until they said they agreed with the Catholic Church—and then they were killed. Simply being called a "witch" was reason to be burned alive or drowned. A Jew or a Moslem was in danger his entire life. Anybody who questioned Christianity was called a "heretic" or a "blasphemer" and was punished cruelly. The land was full of both faith and fear.

The process of seeking out and punishing

heretics was known as "the Inquisition." It had gone on for decades and was led by Catholic Church officials. There was no separation of church and state in Spain. Churchmen were in charge of writing the laws and enforcing them. Anyone who disagreed was silenced.

Cristóbal had seen hangings and tortures in his own market square in Genoa. He had watched fellow sailors be whipped bloody with cat-o'-nine-tails onboard ships. The strict rules of Spain were only a bit harsher than those he was used to. Besides, Pope Alexander VI agreed with all of it. It must be right. The Spanish authorities were just trying to keep the country safe for good Christians.

Cristóbal began to look forward to his meeting with Antonio's friend. These were people he understood. He had learned that the count of Medina Celi was one of the most important landowners in Spain. He was also the owner of a large merchant fleet. This man could finance "The Enterprise" himself, if he wanted.

The count listened to Cristóbal's ideas with gathering excitement. He called in experts and worked out the figures. Perhaps the earth was as small as Cristóbal thought, after all. If so, this was a wonderful idea. Cristóbal was thrilled. Here was his sponsor!

But the count of Medina Celi was a realist. He had lived in Spain all his life. He knew that the king and queen would have to be involved in anything this important. The last thing he wanted was to anger the monarchs. Like everyone, he was afraid of their ruthless power.

"Cristóbal," he finally admitted, "I cannot be your patron." Before Cristóbal could ask why, the count said, "You should present your ideas at the royal court instead." He pulled a parchment from his cloak. It was sealed with wax and tied with ribbons. "I will give you this letter of introduction to the queen. She will like you. She is bright, adventurous, and about your age. And, of course, she is a devout Christian." The count clapped his hand on Cristóbal's shoulder. "You two should get along fine. God be with you!"

Cristóbal left, full of hope.

CHAPTER EIGHT
QUEEN ISABELLA

"No," said the king. Cristóbal had waited a year for an invitation to speak with King Ferdinand and Queen Isabella. He had made his best arguments. The king refused to waste his time on this Genoese dreamer. The queen had seemed more interested.

"Your Highness," Cristóbal pleaded. The sharp crack of the queen's fan and the rustle of her stiff brocade dress stopped him. Guards on both sides stepped forward, but she waved them away.

"I know your arguments, Cristóbal Colón," she said, "and they are good ones. You would bring such glory to Spain. If"—she shook her head firmly—"if I could, I would take your enterprise on as my own. Now, however, is not the time."

Before Cristóbal could ask why, she went on. "We are in the midst of a war—a war we are winning. We will chase the Moors out of Spain in a few more months. Then we will purify the entire country. Perhaps after that . . ."

"Then there is still hope, Your Highness?" Cristóbal's heart rose.

"Oh, indeed." The Queen laughed and fluttered her fan. "I do enjoy your spirit. Yes, yes, I approve of your plan. Someday, perhaps . . ."

Cristóbal's breath caught. *She approved?* That was as close as he had gotten. How long could he afford to wait? He thought quickly of his finances.

"I will provide you with a small fund," she said. "I shall enjoy seeing you around the court." The guards motioned that the audience was over, but Cristóbal stole one last look at the red-haired, blue-eyed queen before he bowed. She believed in his dream! She wanted to see him again! He could almost feel the Ocean Sea breeze against his face already.

While Cristóbal waited near the royal family in Córdoba, he met a young woman from home. Beatriz Enríquez de Arana came from a poor Genoese family of farmers. She was thrilled to know the handsome Cristóbal Colón, a trades-man who had married into nobility. The fact that he knew Queen Isabella in person was incredible to this farm girl. He was an explorer, too, and a dreamer. In a few months he would be sailing to the Orient. How his blue eyes burned when he talked about it!

For Cristóbal, Beatriz was the answer to his lonely prayers. He could not marry her, of course. She was beneath him in society now.

They decided to live together, as many others did in the Spanish court at the time. They moved often while Cristóbal followed the queen. She and the entire royal court moved every season. Moving every season had its advantages for the king and queen. They could keep an eye on all of their subjects, visit all of the royal palaces, parks, and properties possible, and avoid the worst winter weather and summer heat, too.

At Cristóbal's first chance, he made his case again. "I will bring you glory," he told the queen. "I will risk my life for you and for the Catholic Church." Cristóbal knew how she and the king valued their title of the Catholic monarchs. The pope himself had given that title to them for their loyalty. Cristóbal described how many thousands of Christian converts she could claim for the pope—and for her God. Over the years, the Spanish Inquisition was becoming ever harsher. The priests in charge had invented horrible torture machines to punish people who did not agree with them. "There is evil here," they said. "The Devil is at work. We are doing God's will by fighting the Devil." They persecuted Jews and Moslems. They could prove that any village herb lady or midwife who questioned their authority was a Devil worshipper, or a witch, or both. The proof? They could get their poor victims to confess—if the torture went on long enough.

"Imagine," Cristóbal told the queen, "a chain of Spanish Catholic colonies spread around the world under your rule. All worshiping under our pope. I would claim all the lands I discover in your name, of course." All he would ask in return for risking his life was a title: "Perhaps admiral of the Ocean Sea? And of course my sons would inherit the title." Cristóbal tried other things to tempt her.

"Imagine all the gold and silver, spices, gems, slaves, and trade goods that would flow through Spain—as well as souls for God." For risking his life, he would ask for no more than 10 percent of the income.

The queen called a committee of the wisest men and priests to decide if Cristóbal's dream was possible. For four and a half years, Spanish scientists, geographers, and priests argued amongst themselves. The king and queen gave Cristóbal barely enough money to live on while he waited. He could not start another business because he had to move so often. In 1488, he and Beatriz had a son, whom they named Ferdinand. Now, Diego, Cristóbal's first son, was a page at court. He served the dons and other royalty, running errands and carrying messages. The Colóns struggled to buy the fancy clothes they needed to wear around royalty. They looked and felt very poor. They had no real home. All they really had was Cristóbal's dream.

Finally, the king's advisers made their decision: "This Cristóbal Colón is mad," the committee report said. "His plan is nonsense."

When King John II of Portugal wrote asking Cristóbal to come to court again, Cristóbal was thrilled. He packed up his sons and Beatriz and headed back to Lisbon. Perhaps this king had changed his mind.

Instead, the king had tricked him into attending a ceremony honoring another explorer, Bartholomew Dias. While the whole crowd watched, Dias drew the course he had sailed on a big map. He had followed the coast of Africa South. He filled in the chart farther than anyone ever had before, describing huge rivers and strange animals he had seen. He produced black-skinned natives he had caught from unknown tribes. Dias showed how he had found a southern end to Africa—and then he had sailed north up the other side.

"Then," Dias said, "my crew gave up in terror. Had we gone on, we could have sailed straight to India. We have good hope that we have finally found the route!"

Cheers filled the great room of the castle. There were many speeches and honors for Bartholomew Dias. King John II named the passage around Africa the Cape of Good Hope. In public, the king showed that Cristóbal's route would be useless now.

Then he heard that King John's tricks went further. The king had copied Cristóbal's secret charts for "The Enterprise of the Indies." Portuguese ships had sailed on his dream voyage already. The king claimed that Cristóbal's maps led them to nothing but wild storms and more ocean.

Cristóbal left the court furious. He stopped to talk with his brother in Lisbon. Bartolo, just as angry, closed the chart-making shop and he booked passage on a ship bound for England. He planned to talk with the king there, Henry VII, to try to persuade him to finance Cristóbal's voyage.

Cristóbal sailed back to Spain to haunt the royal court again. Only the king had said "no." Queen Isabella had once said "perhaps . . ." She had not insulted him the way King John had, either.

For the next year, Cristóbal was poorer than ever. He followed the queen wherever she went. His dream, "The Enterprise," filled his waking and sleeping hours. Mid-year, he heard that his brother's boat was either lost, ship-wrecked, or taken by pirates. England's King Henry VII never heard Cristóbal's plan. Isabella was his only hope now. There was other news. The Spanish fight against the Moors was going well. The Inquisition was finding and killing many nonbelievers. Cristóbal felt his time was coming.

On January 2, 1492, Ferdinand and Isabella fought—and won—the last great battle against the Moors. Granada surrendered. For seven hundred years, the Moslems had ruled in Spain. Now, at last, everyone in the country would be Roman Catholic like its king and queen.

There was wild, joyous celebrating in the streets. Bells rang from every chapel, monastery, convent, and cathedral. Cristóbal once again tried to get the queen to pay attention to his dream.

"I would risk my life for the glory of Spain," he said, "and for the Faith."

"But there is one more thing we must do here," she said. The Catholic monarchs announced that every last Moslem and Jew had to leave the country. Many of Spain's doctors and astronomers, professors and navigators were Jews or Moors. That didn't matter. It didn't count that their families had lived in Spain for centuries. Only those who worshipped Christ exactly as the pope decreed could stay. Anyone else would be killed.

Cristóbal left a month later. He had heard enough. Isabella was never going to help him. Penniless, he rode a mule and then walked toward the coast. All was lost. The dust of the road settled in his mouth and clung to his cloak, but Cristóbal plodded on, away from his dream.

Halfway across a bridge, in the little seaside village of Pinos, he heard hoofbeats behind him on the road. Cristóbal moved to one side to let the rider hurry by, but the horse pulled up beside him. A messenger leaned down. "The queen," he panted, "the queen."

Cristóbal grabbed the horse's bridle. "Make sense, man," he demanded.

"Your 'Enterprise of the Indies'?" the lad stammered. "Her Majesty wishes you to begin it at once."

The rest of the tale is well documented. We have copies of Columbus's ship's logs. Ferdinand Columbus wrote down his father's story. So did other writers in the 1500s. In the centuries since then, research historians have filled in many of the details.

★ ★ ★

CHAPTER NINE

THE OCEAN SEA

The great Enterprise began with a flurry of paperwork. On April 17, 1492, King Ferdinand and Queen Isabella signed an agreement with Cristóbal Colón. They had subdued their country. Now they were ready to give him the right to sail the Ocean Sea under the Spanish flag. He would claim his discoveries for Spain. The agreement detailed how much money he would get for his ships and crew. It said what he would get if he were successful. Few believed Cristóbal would even survive.

The queen gave him a letter of introduction to the foreign leaders he might meet. Their names were left blank, of course. No one knew who the leaders were in the Far East. Cristóbal got a passport. That way, as he passed from port to port, he could prove both who he was and from where he had come.

The orders demanded that the little coastal town of Palos provide three fully rigged ships. The royal family wasn't willing to take all the risk. Cristóbal had to use his good name to borrow more funds. He went into debt to Genoa's banks and his friends in the Spanish court to outfit the ships for ocean travel.

The larger, stronger ship would carry the Spanish flag. Cristóbal called his flagship the *Santa María*. It could hold forty men and boys, but only if they slept crowded together, and in shifts. Almost eighty feet long, it would carry Cristóbal as captain.

Two smaller caravels prepared to sail too. These smaller ships would be perfect for exploring coasts and islands. One was called the *Pinta*. The other was called the *Niña*. Cristóbal chose a seaman he trusted to be the *Niña*'s captain.

Vicente Yañez Pinzón was well known and respected in Palos. Once he was hired as an officer, local crewmen began to sign up for the voyage. That left the *Pinta* without a captain. Vicente insisted that his brother, Martín Alonso Pinzón, be hired as the *Pinta*'s captain. Martin was not as nice a man. Everybody knew that, but he was an expert seaman.

The *Niña* carried twenty-four sailors; the *Pinta,* twenty-six. Finding people to sail three boats was not easy. A few skilled people believed in "The Enterprise." A surgeon, carpenters, a silversmith, a few able seamen, and the owner of the *Santa María* signed on. Many other people thought taking the voyage would be suicidal. To fill out the crew, Cristóbal had to include four criminals. They had been pardoned just so they could go on the voyage. One had been condemned to death for killing a man. The other three had tried to help him escape. Several boys who had never been to sea before signed on, just for the adventure.

It took three months to get everything in place. Finally, their sailing date was set for August 3, 1492.

The docks were busy that day. The Spanish Inquisition had decreed that every last Jew and Moslem in all of Spain and its territories had to leave on August 3. It did not matter if they had businesses or fields ready to harvest. Catholics would get their land and homes, their farms and their family graveyards. Jewish and Moslem refugees fleeing for their lives filled the docks. Outgoing ships were crowded with these weeping Spaniards.

In the chapel by the dock in Palos there was only excitement. Cristóbal, his captains, and the crew knelt to receive communion. The priest blessed them and their voyage. It seemed that the weather blessed them, too, for the sky was clear and a stiff breeze filled the sails as the little fleet headed into the unknown.

First, they headed eight hundred miles south toward the Canary Islands. These islands were well settled and on every ocean chart. The boats could stock up on supplies there. They would need fresh meat, cheese, water, and wood for the long voyage ahead. It would also be a good test cruise to make sure the boats were seaworthy.

The boats were not well matched. The *Pinta* and the *Niña* were fast. They often had to pull in their sails and wait for the *Santa María* to catch up. Three days into the trip, Cristóbal saw a smoky distress signal from the *Pinta*. When he pulled up aside it, Martin leaned toward him and yelled, "The rudder. It has come loose!"

Unable to steer, he had to make his way using the wind's direction. It took him three days to get to Grand Canary Island. Cristóbal and Vicente had troubles too. The wind made it impossible to sail into Grand Canary. They landed at Gomera, another of the Canary Islands, instead. There, Cristóbal got provisions. He replaced the lateen sails of the *Niña* with square sails. This new rigging would be much better in high winds on the open sea.

After that, they sailed to Grand Canary. Cristóbal took one look at the rudder repairs and shook his head. "We have to wait while a new rudder is built for the *Pinta*," he announced. It took a month.

On September 9, they set out toward the sunset, heading west into the dusk. By dark, all traces of land had disappeared. The ocean beneath them rolled slowly with waves coming from a distant unknown. The more the men thought about the danger, the more frightened they became. They muttered as they changed shifts. Were they on a fool's errand?

"Be of good cheer," Cristóbal told them. "In only a few weeks we will see land. You all will be heroes." His encouragement did little to stop their complaining. Cristóbal told his first mate to remind the men of the cat-o'-nine-tails onboard. He also started to make two sets of records. One would be accurate; he would keep the true set to himself. To the men, he would show faked charts of slow progress. That way, the crew would not know if the voyage was taking longer than expected.

Cristóbal slept well that night. For the next week, the weather was clear and the wind, steady. Every morning the crew gathered to recite prayers. Every evening they sang "Salve Regina," an ancient hymn of praise to Jesus' mother, Mary. These sailors were devout at these ceremonies, but they did not dress up. The seamen went barefoot. They wore red woolen stocking caps and gray, knee-length, blouse-like shirts, belted at the waist with a sash. They did not bother with a doublet or cloak, chains or hose.

The captains wore these extra clothes on top of their under blouses. They wore soft boots, too. At a glance they looked different from the others. "Here comes the captain!" the men began to whisper after the first month at sea. "Maybe we should heave him overboard and head home!" The wind had dropped, and the water was thick with strange, floating seaweed [modern Sargasso Sea, mid-Atlantic].

The sailors were losing faith in Cristóbal's mission. They had sailed steadily for five weeks, surrounded by an endless sea. The sky always looked the same too. Every day felt the same. They said the same prayers and sang the same songs. For four-hour shifts, they listened to the same *slap-slap-slap* of water against the hull and the creaking of ropes. There were no landmarks to show they had gone anywhere at all.

When the wind picked up again, it was

going the wrong way. Cristóbal took out his fake charts and showed all the seamen how far they had come—and how far they still had to go. "We never expected to see land this close," he lied. "Just wait another week. You will see. And these wonderful winds ·will make the homeward trip quick and easy."

The men grumbled, but they pressed forward. Toward the end of September, tropical birds soared overhead. They had to be heading toward land! On September 25, Martin shouted, "Land ahoy!" from the *Pinta*. Sailors fell to their knees in prayers of thanksgiving. But it was a cruel mistake. After another day's sail, there was still no land to be seen.

Another week passed. The men stopped listening to Cristóbal's stories of wealth and adventure. They wanted to go home. Martin and Vicente came aboard the *Santa María* and told Cristóbal that they were ready to quit too.

Cristóbal fought for his dream as he had for years. "We press on," he said.

The next morning another false "land ahoy" was sounded. It was only a clump of rain clouds in the distance. "Clouds like that form over islands," Martin told Cristóbal. "Turn toward them." Now they sailed in the direction the birds had flown. They headed toward where rain seemed to be falling. Two more days they sailed—and then a third.

The men were wild. The food had gone bad. They had not seen land for a month since leaving the Canaries. They wondered if they would survive. "We are stuck with a madman!" they said. "He will never let us go home!"

Cristóbal made a deal with them. "I know we will see land in the next two or three days. If not, we will turn around and go home.

"Look lively, now. The first man who sees land will get a reward of ten times a month's pay." The sailors had forgotten about the money. Everyone wanted that prize. They began to see small things in the water: a twig with green leaves, a flower, a carved stick. It seemed that land had to be close, but where *was* it?

CHAPTER TEN
LAND HO!

At sunset on the seventy-first day, the breeze picked up into a gale, driving the ships in front of it. The clouds blew off, and the stars shone brightly. After the crew sang "Salve Regina," Cristóbal strode to the front of the *Santa María*. He gazed at a bright quarter moon, then scanned the dark horizon. The land had to be there *somewhere*.

A tiny flicker of light caught his eye. Cristóbal stood rigid. A *candle*? He saw it again. A flare from a boat that was sardine fishing, perhaps? "You," he called to a sailor nearby, "look yonder. Is that a signal?"

The sailor, Pedro Gutiérrez, was a servant of the king. He hurried to Cristóbal's side. "Nay," he said. But he stared along Cristóbal's outstretched arm into the darkness. "Oh, there it is!" he cried. "I think."

"Rodrigo!" Cristóbal called to one of the accountants who happened nearby. "Are your eyes good? Can you see this light?"

"It was very small," Pedro told his friend. "But I did see it, just for a moment."

No matter how long they stared into the windy night sky, the light did not reappear. They finally gave up and found places to lie down and sleep.

"Land ho! Land ho!" Rodrigo de Triana's cry woke everyone onboard the *Pinta*. The sailor pointed into the night, yelling, "I saw it first! I get the prize!" This was no false landfall. Moonlight showed steep cliffs and glittered in the froth of waves on a pale beach. The cannon blast they set off to celebrate woke everyone on the other ships too. It was only two A.M., but there were prayers and songs.

Between the verses, they could hear the crashing of waves on a reef nearby.

"Drop anchors!" Cristóbal ordered. For the first time in two months, the sailors heard the sound of anchor chains rattling through their fittings. "We claim this land on the morrow."

The officers opened sea chests and shook out their brocade doublets, fine hose, and fancy fur-collared cloaks. Gold chains and dress swords, heavy rings, and official documents had to be located. Armor needed to be buffed to a shine. In the morning they would finally see the Oriental palaces with gold roofs. There would be beautiful princesses in silks and jewels. They would claim the land and untold riches. They had to look good. They would represent all of Spain.

At last, the banners were ready. Metal shone and leather gleamed. The heavy crosses were attached to their wooden staffs and polished. At last, everything was ready for the ceremony—except daylight.

* * * *

Rough winds and seas greeted them at dawn. They weighed anchor and sailed toward the land, anyway. A pale sweep of sandy beach and palm trees lay empty in the early light. The Indies looked nothing like Marco Polo had described. There were no crowds of people, exotic-looking buildings, or thriving markets. There were only a few naked savages peeking at them from behind trees. The sailors did not care. They had finally reached land!

The boats circled westward looking for safe anchorage. At last they found a break in the reef and moved into a small harbor. Cristóbal and the other officials climbed into rowboats and went to shore with Spanish banners flying.

The islanders watched from the shelter of trees. They stared at these hairy-faced strangers. "Where did they come from?" one of the natives asked in his own language. No one could remember a tribe that wore such strange clothing.

Why would they cover their bodies when the sun burned hot? Even the elder, who had paddled to dozens of islands, had no answer. They watched silently as the strangers fell to their knees and kissed the ground. The men wept like children. Then they stabbed the ground with banners and a tall, shiny symbol. They sang and chanted, but none of their words made sense. They made signs of magic with their hands too. The islanders remembered everything they saw so they could tell the others.

Cristóbal unrolled a parchment and claimed the island in the name of the Catholic sovereigns of Spain. "This island will be called San Salvador," Cristóbal's voice rang out. The crewmen all crossed themselves at this. An island named Holy Savior reminded them of their second reason for sailing so far. First was wealth and glory, of course. Second was to bring the faith to these heathens. This would be easy. One of the natives had already mimicked their moves of touching forehead, then chest, shoulder and shoulder. Another gazed at the shiny gold cross glittering in the tropical sun. "Your land has a new king and queen," Cristóbal said, taking care to speak very slowly and loud.

"San Salvadore," he said, stretching his arm to show the whole of their island.

The natives looked at one another in surprise. It looked as if the stranger was pointing at their island, but he kept repeating an odd word for it. It would be rude to disagree directly. Finally, one spoke. "Guanahani," he corrected politely, waving at their home. He walked across the beach to greet these friendly newcomers.

"How can their skin be so pale?" his brother asked. "Why don't they paint their faces?" His friends followed, staring at Cristóbal's red hair and beard, at the stranger's glittering swords, and at the sharp metal points on the ends of their long staffs.

One of the strangers pulled the hat off his own head and offered it.

"Careful!" the elder said.

The youngest islander took it. "Woven," he said. "But it's not made of sweet grass or bark fiber!" He sniffed it. "Sweat and animal hair." He pulled it on his head, since the stranger was showing him how. "Too hot on a day like this," he said. He took it off again. "It might make a good carrying pouch, though. Or a sack for a tiny baby."

"Oh, now they want to give us beads!" the elder said, taking a handful from one of the strangers. He looked at the gifts closely, then nodded at his tribesmen. Everyone who took the necklaces had something to say about their startlingly clear stones. "Think my girlfriend will finally be impressed with me?" one asked, posturing. "Never," came the answer, and they all laughed. "Will the chief take a portion of these in tax?" one wondered. Another said he would ask his wife to sew these beads into the sacred pattern on his ceremonial robe. "Better to unstring these beads," an islander suggested, "so all the tribes members can share the wealth." The natives tried to calculate the value of a single bead used in trade with the tribes from other islands.

Cristóbal watched the natives. "We've reached the Indies," he told his crewmates. "These copper-skinned Indians are simpkins, all of them. Look how childlike they are, jibbering and chattering like monkeys over these worthless trinkets. They do not even know to cover their nakedness before God."

He unsheathed his sword and showed it to one native. The Indian reached out to touch the strange silvery substance and pulled his hand back. Blood flowed from a cut on his hand. His tribesmen hissed in sympathy. "Never seen steel," Cristóbal said. "We have nothing to fear here."

He waved for the other sailors to come ashore. They brought other trade trinkets. The islanders exclaimed over tiny mirrors and rang the shiny metal hawk bells. "Do you think they tame falcons to hunt with them like the royals do?" the first mate asked. Cristóbal snorted at the mate's foolishness.

Some of the islanders ran off, but they returned quickly. They had bright colored parrots riding on their wrists. These birds seemed happy to sit on the sailors' shoulders, too. Other islanders offered skeins of woven cloth. Cristóbal fingered the material with amazement. The weave was fine, and the cloth was soft as linen. A pattern was woven into the fabric. Clearly these simple Indians could not have made it themselves. There must be trade routes here linking them with the great kahns. Another native tried to hand his men old shards of broken pottery.

"Look at that!" the youngest said. "He threw my gift on the ground!" The other islanders backed away. "Doesn't he know this clay was mined by our ancestors?" the boy went on. "Their sacred hands milled it, then formed it, painted it, and then fired it." Anger made his tongue loose. "These fur-faced men could have ground the pieces again. The new pottery would hold history of untold seasons. And these ignorant strangers thought them worthless!" The islanders shifted uneasily. The visitors seemed to have no manners, but neither did their own child.

"Do you have this?" Cristóbal stared at the natives, and then pointed at the cross. "Gold?" He then pointed at his ring, necklace, and medallion. "Where is your gold?" Cristóbal asked again.

Cristóbal considered the Indians uncivilized, while the Indians thought the sailors were too unintelligent to understand. Cristóbal called his men together. "We go back to the boats tonight," he said. "We will look for more islands tomorrow—and for Cipango [modern Japan] itself. We must find gold." Cristóbal's debts were huge, and he had promised the queen great wealth. He intended to claim the prize for sighting land—he had seen the light first, after all. But that was not enough. It was nowhere near enough. He pointed again at his necklace.

The oldest Indian stepped closer, trying to understand. He stared at the medallion and then pointed at the golden sun to the west. "Ah-ha!" Cristóbal said. "The natives do have gold. This old one will show us where it is. Take him." Suddenly a handful of the sailors surrounded the elder and pushed him toward the rowboats. He turned to rejoin his friends, but the magical silver blades cut at his skin. More strangers crowded around him until he was dizzy with the stink of them and he fell backward into the wooden boat.

The Spaniards sailed to another island they could see on the horizon. One Indian had a gold nose ring. The sailors spread out over the island. They found thatch-roofed huts, with man-size nets hanging inside where the Indians slept. They found rain-collecting channels and cisterns, too. There were no freshwater springs where they could restock the ships' supplies. And there was no palace full of treasure. There was no gold mine. "Take him!" Cristóbal said before they left. "Don't hurt him. We'll use the savage as a navigator or a translator. Or maybe he can just carry my cap." Cristóbal and his men did not think the natives' lives were as precious as their own.

The explorers visited island after island. Everywhere they went, Cristóbal demanded an answer about where to find gold. Everywhere, the Indians were friendly at first and tried to be helpful. Even when they understood what this off-islander was asking for, they could not help him. All islanders knew there was very little gold in the world. Finally they would all resort to pointing somewhere else to get the furry-faced sailors to go away.

The fleet sailed on for three days and found land [modern Cuba]. "The Indies!" Cristóbal said. "We are here!"

He was wrong. Cristóbal's discovery was far grander than he'd imagined. He'd thought he was revisiting the country Marco Polo had known so well. Instead, he had landed on a vast continent new to his people. He had spent most of his life trying to get to the Indies, so that was all he could think of. Even when the evidence did not fit, he clung to his dream.

When Cristóbal asked to see the gold, the natives in this new land pointed to the mountains. "You," he said, waving at some of his men, "form an exploring party. Head inland. Find that gold and return here in six days." The men streaked off, glad to be the first to get their hands on gold.

"The rest of you can relax, finally," Cristóbal said. The remaining sailors made repairs on their boats. The friendly natives gave them gifts of food. The seamen tried sweet potatoes, a yellow grain the Indians called "maize," and fat red beans shaped like kidneys. Cristóbal listened closely when the natives talked. He was trying to learn their language. He also wanted to learn how to find the cities Marco Polo saw.

He thought he heard the Indians use words that sounded something like "Cathay" or "Cipango" or "kahn." *"The Enterprise of the Indies"* was right on track, he told himself. "This is just a peninsula off Cathay," he told everyone else.

The exploring party came back from the

interior. There was just an Indian village of fifty huts there, they said. The Indians smoked pipes full of a strange weed they called "tobacos," but they had no gold. Cristóbal ordered the capture of another Indian or two, to have something to show the queen and king. Cristóbal thought they would find the uncivilized Indians amusing. Cristóbal and his men sailed on, exploring the coastline. October passed, and November. The weather turned bad, and for days they had to sit at anchor, waiting out drenching rains or howling winds. When they could inch along, they did. In a storm, the *Pinta* sailed away from the other two boats.

Cristóbal was furious. "That Martin Pinzon!" he grumbled. "He is probably out claiming land for himself!"

On December 9, Cristóbal sailed across a channel to another big island. He named this one La Española, or Little Spain [modern

Hispaniola]. It was a beautiful place, with springs and good farmland. It had Indians, of course. Like the others, they seemed to know nothing about gold. Cristóbal sailed on. He met one chief and invited him to dine on the *Santa María*. The man would not eat the entire feast that was prepared to impress him. Instead, he just tasted everything and took the rest back to share with his people.

At a landing they named Santo Tomás, they were met by a gentle tribe.

"Taino," the Indians said, pointing at one another.

"Guacanagari," the chief, said, pressing his hand to his chest. Guacanagari gave Cristóbal a mask that had a hammered gold nose. The Spanish stayed there for a week or more. "Be especially nice to these Tainos. They have gold," Cristóbal told his men. "And later, they'll be easy to convert to Christianity." He knew many of the Indians' words and hand signals now. Everyone was friendly. When the Spaniards left, hundreds of Taino tribe members lined the beaches. They begged the sailors to stay. Cristóbal had to order the ships to leave. There was more exploring to do.

They didn't get far. On Christmas Eve night, the *Santa María* sailed near a jagged coral reef. An unseen current swept them right onto the sharp corals. Suddenly the ship tilted and stopped. The sound of splintering timbers and water gushing through the hull woke everyone. "Abandon ship!" Columbus ordered. All the sailors rowed to the *Niña*, which was floating nearby. They crowded together on the deck and watched the *Santa María* sink.

Cristóbal stood, silent, wrestling with awful questions. How could this have happened to him? What could he do for his men? Would the *Niña* sink tonight, overcrowded like this? How would they ever get home? Where *was* Pinzon and the *Pinta*? They needed help.

Suddenly, Cristóbal remembered: They had a friend here in the Indies!

The next morning, chests and barrels from the *Santa María* floated about. The sea bobbed with timbers and oars, masts and tangled ropes. The crew gathered what they could of the shipwreck. Cristóbal sent a rowboat back to the place they had called Santo Tomás. "Find Chief Guacanagari of the Tainos," he said. "And hurry!"

The chief sped back to the *Niña* with a fleet of canoes. The heathen savage had saved them all! Cristóbal invited the chief to dine with him on the *Niña* in thanks. Every time the chief admired something, Cristóbal gave it to him. By the end of the meal, Guacanagari was the proud owner of a string of amber beads, a big red cloak, and a bottle of orange-flavored water. Cristóbal asked him what else the Spanish could do for him in thanks.

"We do need some help," the chief admitted in sign language and shared words. "A nearby tribe, the Caribs, are fierce hunters. They attack our villages, killing with bows and arrows. Then they eat the bodies of our dead."

"They won't when they know you are under the protection of the Spanish crown!" Cristóbal said. He ordered his best archers to show off their skill with crossbows. The metal-tipped arrows sliced right into wood. Then he had the cannons fired, just for show. The thunderous noise and choking clouds of gunpowder smoke terrified the Indians. "Our might will protect you," Cristóbal promised. Then he pressed Guacanagari for information on gold. Confused, the chief gave the captain the tribe's treasured gold mask. It was a small price to pay for the protection of the Spaniards.

Cristóbal had a hard decision to make. There were more men than he could carry home in the little *Niña*. Now that they had proof of gold here and a tribe of friendly Indians, he knew he would be coming back. He chose thirty-nine men to stay behind and search for the Tainos' gold mine. With the Indians' help, they gathered all the timbers they could from the shipwreck. They used them to build a fort. Cristóbal named it La Navidad, since it had been founded on Christmas Day.

By New Year's day 1493, Spaniards had slept in the first Christian settlement. They had artillery to use against the Caribs if they needed it. They had seedlings to plant for their own food. Cristóbal gave them all the leftover trade goods in case they met with other tribes. The *Niña* was stocked for a long voyage home. It was time to leave. After one last feast, Cristóbal headed home.

The trip began in fine weather. Within days, the *Pinta* was sighted. Her captain, Martin Pinzón, had plenty of excuses, but Cristóbal didn't really care. He needed to get home, and the weather was turning bad. They stopped at one last island to claim it. Instead of being friendly, the Indians there attacked with a shower of arrows. The islanders had blackened their faces with charcoal. They wore high tufts of parrot feathers in their hair. The Spaniards knew these must be Caribs. The sailors fought back and fled out to sea.

The weather only got worse. The *Niña* lost sight of the *Pinta* again. Winter storms lashed the little boat on its long journey across the Ocean Sea. Huge swells threatened to capsize the *Niña*. There was no rest. Night and day, it took everyone's strength just to keep the boat moving in the right direction. There were no morning prayers or evening hymns now. There were only howling gales and buckets of rain, enormous waves, and salt water sprayed into everyone's eyes and mouths. Men had to work the pumps constantly to keep the boat from filling with water.

They were beyond exhaustion. They lived in cold, wet clothes. They had not eaten well in weeks. The loss of nutrients caused sores and weakness. Cristóbal's legs had gone numb. They ached, whether he moved or not. Other sailors were even sicker. The men prayed for God to save them. "If You allow us to get to land," they bargained, "we will go to church before we do anything else." The storm raged on, driving the ship before it.

One day, the fierce wind suddenly shifted. The sun came out. The *Niña* turned her sails. Within hours, a blessed call came from above: "Land ho!"

They were almost home! These were the Azore Islands. They had been discovered, claimed, and settled by Portugal. Cristóbal looked up at the tattered Spanish flag flapping from the *Niña*'s mast. He knew it was not wise to stop at a Portuguese port. Spain and Portugal were always feuding. But his men desperately needed fresh food and water. They needed to get dry and warm. "Drop anchor!" he ordered after they entered the harbor.

The sailors crowded into rowboats, cheering with joy. They staggered from the dock to a nearby chapel. It was cozy there, dim and blessedly dry. Every sailor sank to his knees before the altar. The warmth and sweet smell of incense were enough to make Cristóbal weep. Instead, he prayed.

Suddenly the chapel doors swung open. Portuguese soldiers tramped in and grabbed the sailors. Knives and guns flashed, but the exhausted men were no match for the soldiers. No one had time to say "amen."

"You are under arrest, Spanish dogs!" the commander growled, and hurried them out into the harsh winter sunshine.

CHAPTER ELEVEN

ADMIRAL OF THE OCEAN SEA

"But I am Cristóbal Colón! I am a Spanish subject and represent the Spanish crown!" The soldiers just laughed and hauled Cristóbal and his sailors to the local magistrate. He looked at Cristóbal's passport.

"It is indeed a royal pass," he said, astonished, "signed by the king and queen of Spain!" He allowed the weary captain and crew to go on. "I do not want to start a war here on this island."

"Hoist sail!" Cristóbal ordered. "Make use of every bit of wind!" They sped toward Spain. *What if Martin Pinzón has beaten me to court? What if he has claimed the glory, the title, and the reward money?* The thought of the *Pinta*'s sneaky captain burned in Cristóbal's mind. When the breeze began to rise, the *Niña*'s sails strained, pushing them homeward. Cristóbal's hopes rose with the wind. However, that wind whipped into a sudden wild storm. The masts creaked under the stress. The sails bulged and strained. The ropes stretched almost to breaking. "Drop the sail!" Cristóbal shrieked into the howling gale. His men tried to ease the sails down. They could not move fast enough. The mainsail split and hung flapping from the rigging.

When the storm died, the men raised the few sails that were still in one piece. "Head for the nearest port," Cristóbal said. "That's all we can do now."

"But that lands us in Portugal!" his helmsman said. "We'll be back in Portuguese jails!"

"I'll write to King John and ask his permission to make repairs in his country. We will promise to set sail immediately." Cristóbal's spirits rose as his success settled in. "Why, it will be an honor for him to host us. We found the trade route."

King John II made Cristóbal come to court and face him. He tried to claim Cristóbal's discovery for Portugal. "You lived in Portugal first, after all," he said. There was even talk in court about killing Cristóbal. That way, Spain would have no great explorer to brag about.

Finally, they decided to let Cristóbal go, unharmed. He rushed to his boat. Her sail had been repaired, so he wasted no more time. He *had* to get to Queen Isabella before Martin Pinzón did!

On March 15, 1493, seven and a half months after setting sail for the Indies, Cristóbal sailed back into the harbor at Palos, Spain. The *Pinta* was already there. She was lying at anchor. Cristóbal rushed up to the dock. "Where is that snake, Pinzón?" he asked. The news was strange.

Martin Pinzón had beaten him, it was true. However, Ferdinand and Isabella had refused to talk to him. They wanted to reward Cristóbal first. When Pinzón heard that, he gave up and went home. Pinzón had gone to bed, a broken man. A few days later, he was dead.

Cristóbal crossed himself, feeling a mixture of sorrow and guilty relief. "And now, you must hurry to court," the dock master said. He handed Cristóbal a royal summons. It was addressed to "Don Cristóbal Colón, Admiral of the Ocean Sea and Governor of the Islands." It told him to come to Barcelona. He was supposed to plan for another voyage to the Indies, too.

Cristóbal still believed he had discovered islands near the mainland of today's China. How could he think anything else? No one had any idea that there were two vast unknown continents on the earth, full of people and riches. It was beyond Cristóbal's imagination.

He wrote to the king and queen and described his adventure in glowing words. "When I go to the Indies again, I want to settle three or four new Spanish towns there. I will need to bring two thousand volunteers. For each town I will need administrators, too. I will need friars and priests to convert the Indians and teach them the Lord's ways." He even wrote out a set of rules for trading between the colony and Spain.

He set out for Barcelona, eight hundred miles away. The letter got to court before he did. The news of his return to Spain spread even faster.

Crowds gathered all along the road, cheering. Cristóbal sat tall and proud on the back of a mule, waving at everyone. Crew members and wagons trailed after him. A half dozen captured Indians stumbled along in chains. The few Indians who survived the voyage were dressed in feathers, beads, and paint. They wore a few scraps of cloth for modesty. The Europeans stared at the strange heathens. They had never seen anyone like them before. The Indians tried not to react. Many people reached out to poke them to see if they were real. They even pinched the copper-colored skin to see if these natives felt pain. There were cages full of captive parrots to stare at too. Hidden in the wagon, Cristóbal brought a few souvenirs for the queen and king, and a small sample of gold.

On the way to court, Cristóbal stopped to see his sons, Diego and Ferdinand. Now they had a hero for a father.

A grand procession formed around him as he arrived in court. Trumpets blared, and soldiers strutted in dress uniforms. The colorful costumes of noblemen and church leaders filled the throne room. The king and queen rose to their feet to greet him. He bowed low, then knelt to kiss their hands. Everyone gasped when the queen took his hand and raised him to his feet. "Don Cristóbal," she said, pointing to a seat next to the royal throne.

The noblemen stared as Cristóbal actually sat beside the monarchs. He was even allowed to leave his hat on his head. Every other man there was sitting lower than the rulers. They had to take off their caps in respect. Cristóbal was presented with the new coat of arms that would forever identify his family. The queen announced, "Both of Don Cristóbal's sons, Ferdinand and Diego, will carry the title of 'Don' too."

Cristóbal showed the prizes he had brought back with him. One of the Tainos had died on the way to Barcelona. The others had learned to speak some Spanish. Cristóbal reassured the queen that these Indians would make good servants and slaves for working farms and gold mines. Or, if she wanted, he would bring back a supply for her own use in Spain. The Europeans had such a low opinon of the natives that they felt they could be traded like the other goods they found abroad.

"These simple folk will be easy to convert to Christianity, Your Majesty, since they have no religion of their own." No one noticed that the Indians' heads jerked in surprise. Of course the Indians had their own religion. But these Europeans felt that the only real religion was Christianity. They were watching as Cristóbal presented the gold he had collected.

The king and queen discussed the plans Cristóbal had made for his next trip. They brought up a problem: Were his claims going to last? King Henry of Portugal was arguing that the lands belonged to him. He had heard of Cristóbal's "Enterprise" first, years earlier. He had heard of its success first, too, when Cristóbal had landed there.

The Spanish royals decided to ask the pope,

Alexander VI. His Holiness claimed that all lands not already under Catholic rule were his. The pope could give them away to any king or queen he chose.

While they waited for his answer, Don Cristóbal stayed at the court. They gave banquets for him every night. He told his stories over and over. He also got to spend time with Beatriz. With his new wealth, he bought her all the fancy dresses she wanted.

He wrote a report of his discoveries. It included the Indians, the new plants and animals, and the gold. He said the beautiful islands were right off the coast of Cathay. The men he left behind on the Oriental peninsula were already mining gold. His glowing words were printed in a pamphlet. It was sold all over Spain. Then it was reprinted in other languages. Portuguese and Genoans learned of his glory. Florence—Genoa's rival city-state in Italy—published the newsletters in Italian.

The Britians, too, and the Germans, discovered that there were islands far to the west over the Ocean Sea. Now, everyone knew the name Cristóbal Colón, the man who had found a new trade route to the Indies!

By May of 1493, Pope Alexander VI announced that the islands did belong to Spain. So did any lands ever found to the west of them. He allowed Portugal a strip of the Ocean Sea to the east, where King Henry could claim any lands he found.

Five months after his glorious return, Cristóbal was heading out again for a second voyage. Everyone knew it. This time he would land in the grand cities of Cathay or Cipango. He would come home with boats full of gold and spices and fabulous stories from the Orient.

CHAPTER TWELVE

A HERO SAILS

Hundreds of men volunteered to sail with the admiral of the Ocean Sea. They longed for adventure. They wanted the honor of saving souls for God. Mostly they hungered to find gold, even though private trade was banned by the royalty. Officially, one eighth of all the profits found in the East were to go to Don Cristóbal. The Spanish crown claimed all the rest. That was the agreement, but men still dreamed of finding their own fortunes.

They also thought about the Indians they might meet there. The Catholic monarchs of Spain had demanded that they be treated "well and honorably." They believed every soul converted to Christianity added to Spain's glory. Brutality would only make Spain look bad. Even if the natives simply became slaves, the monarchs did not want their workforce treated badly.

Cristóbal had a new title now: captain of the Fleet. He would have seventeen ships under his command. For luck, he called his new flagship the *Santa María*. The old *Niña* would sail again. Most of the volunteers signed on as seamen, laborers, farmers, and miners. Cristóbal's youngest brother, Diego, was going along. So was a doctor and two friars, eager to work with the natives. Cristóbal told them the Indians were "very ripe to be converted to the Holy Catholic faith." None of the Pinzón family was sailing this time. A young Juan Ponce de León was coming, along with handfuls of Cristóbal's friends. The three or four Indian captives who were still alive were brought to be translators.

Juan de Fonseca, the quartermaster, was in charge of keeping track of the men and provisions. Guard dogs protected the cargoes. There were sheep and horses aboard, too. The settlers planned to breed these animals on the islands. They would provide food, wool, and horsepower.

On September 25, 1493, a huge ceremony at the dock at Cádiz was held in their honor. Cheering Spaniards filled the dock. Cristóbal's two boys waved good-bye. Then, the fleet sailed out toward the Canary Islands to stock up before crossing the Ocean Sea.

They paused only a week and a half, then headed west toward the Far East. Don Cristóbal gave each ship captain directions to get to La Navidad. After being tricked by Martin Pinzón, this time the admiral of the Ocean Sea was more careful. Each of his captains got directions in sealed envelopes to the island. Each captain could break the wax seal only if lost from his fleet. Only then could he learn the secret trade route.

Cristóbal led the fleet farther south than he had on his last voyage. He thought that would bring him closer to Cathay—or at least to more islands. More gold would make "The Enterprise" worthwhile.

Three weeks later, the fleet sighted a mountainous island. Since there was no place to land, they sailed on. "Where are the riches we were promised?" some of the men grumbled. The ships landed next on an island that Cristóbal named Guadeloupe. The men relaxed, eating fresh food and drinking their fill of water. A rumor began to pass from man to man: "The gold is in the mountains." Some of the men rushed off toward the inland peaks.

The fleet waited for days for them to return. "They must be lost," the seamen said. At last,

Cristóbal sent search parties. The rescuers found deserted Carib huts. They also found native bodies that had been cut up for their meat. It was the remains of a Carib feast. Sickened, the Spaniards went hunting for the cannibals.

They found a few Caribs in the woods. Their skin was dark, but painted bright red. Their hair was shaven clean on one side of their heads and braided on the other. It took many sailors to overpower them. These natives fought "like lions in chains." They did not give up, either. The Caribs struggled on the rowboats and fought when they got back to the ships, too.

Four days later the "lost" men wandered back down onto the beach. They had not found any gold. They had captured twelve beautiful teenage Arawak girls. They loaded their human treasure onboard and sailed on.

At another island, Cristóbal's men captured more Arawak girls and boys, too. These unlucky children had been the prisoners of Caribs. The cannibals were out on another raiding party. The sailors put their rescued slaves back on their boats. Then, a long Carib canoe streaked around a point in the water.

The Spaniards stared. The Caribs simply froze. Four men, two women, and a boy sat totally still in the canoe for a full hour. The Spaniards thought the Indians were too over-whelmed with awe to move. The Caribs were actually using a well-known hunting trick. The men in these huge canoes were not giving up. They were waiting for their enemies to relax. On a signal, the Caribs shot their arrows when the crew least expected it.

They wounded one Spaniard and killed another.

It did not take long for all the sailors to

attack the Caribs. One of the Caribs had been cut with a sword. "Throw him overboard," someone said. "He's going to die, anyway."

The sailors lined the railing to watch him drown. Instead, the Carib swam away. "Brave fool," someone said. "These Indians have courage." They killed the native with arrows, but their respect lingered. The Indians fought fiercely for their freedom, to defend their friends, and to defeat their enemies. The Spaniards learned this the hard way.

They visited several islands, and then came to La Navidad. Cristóbal hoped for a hearty welcome by the colony of men he'd left behind on the first voyage. He imagined a prospering gold mine, a busy fort, and some fresh converts among the natives. His ships dropped anchor in the familiar harbor. They fired a cannon and flares to announce their return, and waited. No one greeted them.

Instead, Cristóbal saw four dead settlers lying in the bushes.

His old Indian friend, Chief Guacanagari, sent some natives out a canoe. They welcomed the Spaniards with gifts of golden masks. "The chief did not want to come," his interpreters told Cristóbal. The sailors spent the night on the boat wondering what had happened—and why the chief wouldn't greet Cristóbal.

The next morning, they hurried to the fort. It had been burned to the ground. All forty settlers were found nearby, dead.

Cristóbal found Guacanagari. "You sent me gifts. Thank you," he said, and gave the chief trinkets in return. "But what happened here?"

"I tried to stop them. Your men acted like animals." Cristóbal stiffened at the insult from a heathen Indian. "They fought with each other. They wanted gold, so they took my tribesmen and forced them to search for it." Cristóbal nodded. That made sense. "They took our wives and daughters, too, to warm their beds." Cristóbal nodded again. The settlers had been lonely, after all. "I kept my people from fighting back," the chief said. "The neighboring chief was not so patient."

Cristóbal was furious—but not because of what his men had done to the Indians. The settlers had found no gold! Now, Cristóbal believed that Indians could not be trusted. He vowed to remember that. He would seek gold elsewhere.

He buried the settlers and sailed away. The ships landed this time on a lovely site, low and by a river. "La Isabela," Cristóbal declared, planting a cross in the soft ground. Some of the men were sent up into the mountains to scout for traces of gold. The rest built houses and a fortress wall around the new Isabela.

Within days, a tropical rainstorm flooded

the lowlands. The heat was unbearable. A huge crop of mosquitoes bred in the swampy area and drove the settlers half mad. Everything was wet and muddy. The food they found was foreign to their taste.

"Gold! Look!" The scouts were back in a week. In their hands were a few flecks of the precious metal. "It is in the mountain streams," they said. "There must be a huge deposit nearby."

More rains fell before a mining party could head up into the hills. The Spaniards muttered about Columbus: "He promised a fair country-side and gold." "Aye, and instead we got a hot, stinking swamp and mosquitoes." The settlers were exhausted and malnourished. Illness swept La Isabela. With several hundred sick men, Cristóbal needed help.

He sent twelve ships back to Spain with a message for the king and queen. It said that gold had been found. "We need a few more ships," he requested, "full of fresh food, medicine, more clothing, and mules." Cristóbal also asked for a hundred experienced miners.

"Help is coming," he told the angry settlers. He took fifty healthy men up into the mountains to build a new mining town called Santo Tomás. They only found tiny grains of gold. Cristóbal was frantic. He needed to find gold! He owed money to the banks and his friends back home. He owed Ferdinand and Isabella, too. He did not want to be thrown into debtors' prison. He wanted to be a hero—a famous explorer. Doubts clouded his mind. This place did not look anything like Marco Polo had described.

He went back down to La Isabela. "We want to go home," the men told him. They were miserable—and now they were dying. The sickness was worse than anyone had thought. "Take us home," they pleaded. Cristóbal himself longed to return to Spain. There, he was a hero. They held parades for him and feasts of endless, delicious food. He wore clean clothes and gold chains. They called him "Don Cristóbal." No one called him that here anymore.

The crew was restless. One of the men had stolen from some Indians. Soon, others followed his example. The Indians tried to steal back what was theirs. The Spaniards raided Indian villages to punish them. Settlers took anything they wanted. The natives tried to get their property back. "The savages stole from us!" the settlers wailed to Columbus. "Do something about those Indian thieves!"

So Columbus did something. He had several Indians rounded up. Then he had their hands cut off.

As he traveled, Cristóbal's reaction to the

Indians he met continued to be brutal. Some, he attacked with dogs. Others, he shot with crossbows. He took many captives. He had to have something to show to the queen and king.

Still, the men complained. They did not trust Cristóbal anymore—and he did not trust them. Sick of La Isabela, Cristóbal left it under his brother Diego's rule and sailed away with three ships. "We need proof that this is Cathay," he told them all. He explored the southern coastline this time. Where were the gleaming towns and gold-roofed cities that Marco Polo had described? He was frantic. If he failed to find gold, fine cloths, and spices, he was ruined.

The men in his boat began to complain. "You don't have any idea where we are," they challenged. "We want to go home," they said. Among themselves, they muttered, "He is mad."

Cristóbal was sure that the proof he needed was just around the corner. But he could not convince the men to sail on. "Sign this," he said, "and I'll have the proof I need." The oath they signed said that they had reached Asia. They were promising to lie. "Men who break this oath now," he said, "will pay a huge fine and have their tongues cut out. Boys will be whipped one hundred times on their bare backs."

Everyone signed the oath. It was the only hope they had of getting home. As the boats turned to head back to Isabela, Cristóbal fell desperately ill. He stayed in bed through storm after storm. He lay abed as they sailed into the dock, too. He had to be carried ashore.

"Well come, brother!" the familiar voice cheered Cristóbal.

"Bartolo! I thought you were dead!" Cristóbal said, and grabbed his younger brother in a bear hug. Bartolo explained that he had escaped the pirates and made his way back to Spain. He had sailed to La Isabela with supply ships. That reunion was the first happy moment Cristóbal had had in a long time. The settlers were frustrated with everything. There was no comfort, no leadership, and no end to this nightmare mission. There was no gold to make it worthwhile. They captured hundreds of Indian slaves and tried to force them to produce gold. "You must give us a hawk's bell full of gold every three moons," they said.

There was not enough gold on the whole island to fill the thimble-size bells. The Indians tried to tell them but the Spaniards refused to believe it. They treated the Indians like slaves. The Spaniards remembered the Inquisition. They tortured Indians the same way that the Catholic Church had punished non-believers back home. Cristóbal and his men made the laws and enforced them too. Beheadings, hangings, and brandings were normal forms of justice in the 1490s. Because the Spaniards were so frustrated, their tempers were short—and the Indians paid for it.

The natives had never seen any tribe as savage as these Spaniards. Men, women, and children were forced to labor. The slaves tried to escape, but the Spanish had guns and crossbows, dogs, and metal swords. Many natives decided that the only escape from a slow, cruel death was to kill themselves quickly and cleanly.

The settlers still prayed at daily devotions. They sang the "Salve Regina" hymn at night. They felt they were still good Roman Catholics. No one bothered to baptize any of the Indians now. No souls were there to save, the Spaniards told themselves. That way, torturing the heathens was no sin.

Sometimes Cristóbal seemed to remember their Divine Majesty's rule to treat the natives "well and honorably." He would tell the settlers to have mercy. But what could he do? He had lost all control over the men. His reputation was being destroyed, he knew, by reports that sailors brought home. His dream had come to nothing.

His trip home began as a nightmare too. Cristóbal asked the men to capture thirty able-bodied Indians to give to Ferdinand and Isabella. Instead, the settlers went on a savage spree, torturing and executing hundreds of islanders. A hurricane hit before they left the island. Of the dozen ships, only the tough little *Niña* survived the storm. There was just enough wreckage left to piece together one more ship. The sailors crowded their slaves into these two boats and set sail on March 11, 1496. The slaves were naked, cold, and even hungrier than the crew was. Nearly all of them died before reaching Spain. Their bodies were thrown into the sea. On June 11, 1496, the *Niña* and her companion ship entered the Spanish port of Cádiz.

There was no cheering this time. There were no parades. Don Cristóbal Colón, admiral of the Ocean Sea and governor of the islands, wore only a plain monk's robe as he shuffled ashore. He was sick—and he was sorry. Cristóbal knew he had failed both the Crown and the Church.

CHAPTER THIRTEEN
ADMIRAL OF THE MOSQUITOES

Cristóbal trudged to the home of a friend in Cádiz, Father Bernaldez, to rest. He gave his papers and logbooks to Bernaldez. His friend took notes on Cristóbal's stories and nursed him back to health. He also shared some discouraging news.

Another explorer, Vasco da Gama, had led a fleet of four ships all the way around Africa. They had sailed past the Cape of Good Hope and finally landed in India. Da Gama had done what Cristóbal never managed—and he brought back the pepper and cinnamon to prove it. A trade route to the Indies had been found. It was claimed by the Portuguese King John. The race was over. Da Gama had found truly civilized Indians in a city called Calcutta. They had the trade goods there that everyone wanted.

Cristóbal shuffled about in his long brown monk's robe. He had never felt so bad. His body healed slowly. His spirits did too. His "Enterprise of the Indies" was not going well—there was no question about that. He began to think that perhaps he could get his reputation back. He liked being a hero. He still longed for riches. There was still time to convert natives to the true faith. Cristóbal began planning to go back to the Indies, *his* way.

Months after he had sailed into port, Ferdinand and Isabella sent word for him to come to court. This time he had to work much harder to look like a success. Once again, he prepared a parade to demonstrate the glories of the Indies. It had colorful parrots and a string of slaves. Just for display, Cristóbal gave the natives back their gold necklaces and earrings, masks, and bells. He put feather headdresses back on their heads too. He brought along gold dust, flecks, and one precious nugget the size of a thumbnail.

The king and queen welcomed him home. They listened to his glowing stories and admired his displays. Then they read a sealed letter addressed to the monarchs that Cristóbal had brought from one of the settlers. It described how bad the conditions were in Isabella. It showed just how poor an administrator Cristóbal was.

Cristóbal convinced the king and queen that there was still value in his "Enterprise." He just needed another chance to prove it. "Gold and gems are formed closer to the equator," he told them his newest theory. "So I would sail west but even further toward the south. I'll return with the treasures you desire." When they agreed, he told them his plan. "I will need two ships to return at once to

Hispaniola with supplies," he said. "I will need six more to lead in discovery later on."

Finding crews for these ships was harder this time. People had heard about the sickness and swamps, the hunger, hard work, and hurricanes. It was clear now that the settlers would not get rich. Cristóbal had to ask the king and queen to offer pardons to more criminals in exchange for their labor.

On May 30, 1498, a fleet of six boats sailed from Spain. Three went straight to Bartolo, on the island of Hispaniola. They brought supplies and fresh help for the Isabela settlement. Cristóbal's new flagship, *Santa María de Guia*, named after his earlier ships plus three others, sailed south. He hoped to happen on new islands or the mainland of Cathay.

Instead, he sailed into an area of dead calm near the equator. The seas were not boiling, but the air was breathlessly hot. For three weeks the ships sat, sails hanging. Belowdecks, barrels of rum and water burst from the heat and all the stored meat rotted. Above decks, the men suffered, prayed, and complained. What if the wind never blew again?

It did. When their sails finally filled, the ships found land with two huge rivers and three mountain landmarks. "Trinidad" [modern Honduras], Cristóbal claimed for Spain, but he wondered. Rivers that size did not flow on an island. Perhaps he had reached Cathay, Cristóbal thought. But the natives they found still did not look like Orientals. If it wasn't the Indies, what *had* they discovered?

They sailed south along the coastline [modern Nicaragua, Costa Rica, and Panama]. This was clearly no island. And it was not Cathay or Cibango, either.

"I have come to believe," Cristóbal wrote to Ferdinand and Isabella, "that this is a mighty continent which was hitherto unknown . . ." His confidence in discovering the trade route to the Indies was failing. So was his health. He often could not see. However, he could hear. He sailed back to La Isabela. There was no good news there.

"A hundred men have gone up into the mountains," Bartolo told his brother. "They refuse to work for the settlement and for Spain. There are Indians, too, in this rebellion."

Cristóbal sent a letter to the rebel leader. "Dear Friend," it began, but there was no friendship. Demands were made, and agreements broken. Insults, theft, and brutality flared between the camps. There was no peace, though a few of the rebels were allowed to take a couple of ships home. They took stories with them and a sealed note from Cristóbal. The Holy King and Queen were alarmed by what they heard. To find out what was going so wrong with their new territory, they sent a royal officer, Francisco de Bobadilla.

Meanwhile, the secret maps Cristóbal had

made and given to his captains were stolen. Another explorer used them to make his way to Trinidad. Amerigo Vespucci was aboard his ship, taking careful notes. He recognized Cristóbal's discoveries as a whole new continent. He also wrote about it widely. The new land began to be called "America," not "Columbia." Amerigo Vespucci's boat carried home a shipload of slaves, a treasure of pearls from the waters, and a record of reaching this new land.

While he was enroute home, Bobadilla finally arrived in Hispanola to investigate Cristóbal's settlement. Before Amerigo had publicized his new continent, and given it his name, America, Bobadilla finally arrived in Hispanola. The officer was horrified to see two Spaniards hanging from a gallows. Five more were in prisons, awaiting a death sentence. They had plotted to overthrow Cristóbal. Bobadilla listened to the settlers and made his decision. "What was wrong with the settlement?" he asked. The answer he heard everywhere was: "the Colom family: Cristóbal, Bartolo, and Diego."

The Colom family were all arrested, their hands shackled to heavy metal chains. Other chains bound to their ankles kept their movement to a painful shuffle. Bobadilla took the three men home to Spain to present at the court. Onboard ship, he offered to take the irons off his prisoners. There was no escape for them in the middle of the ocean, anyway. Cristóbal's illnesses made wearing chains an extra torture, but he refused to be unshackled.

He shuffled along back in Spain, too, dragging the heavy chains for all to see. "I have been placed in these chains by order of the holy sovereigns," he said to anyone who would listen. "They are the only ones who have the right to take them off."

Cristóbal's sons, Diego and Ferdinand,

were living at the royal court. It was hard to tell which was worse: being called "sons of the Admiral of the Mosquitoes," or seeing their father in chains. When the queen heard about the shackles, she sent word that Cristóbal was to be freed immediately. She sent money for him to buy presentable clothes and insisted that he come to court.

Cristóbal was fifty. His hair had thinned and turned white, and his proud, strong body was bent and weakened by disease. His maps and others' were being copied by chart makers now. Ships for many countries were sailing west across the Ocean Sea and were making new discoveries. The continent of Africa was being explored too. Cristóbal felt left behind. Worse, he felt dishonored. He pleaded for one last trip.

The king and queen sent him out again. In 1502, Cristóbal began his fourth voyage. Four caravels sailed. Cristóbal had been stripped of his titles. He was too weak to be the captain, now. His son Ferdinand was aboard the ship with him. Bartolo and Diego, Cristóbal's brothers, sailed on another ship. At the same time, a supply convoy set out to the Spanish settlements with Bobadilla along. He was supposed to spy on Cristóbal and report back to the king.

From the beginning, this voyage was disastrous. A hurricane struck within days. The supply ships, twenty in all, sank. Bobadilla drowned when his ship went down. Cristóbal's little fleet survived, badly battered. Storms and gales followed them across the Ocean Sea, ripping sails and soaking the food stores. Cristóbal refused to turn back, though his crew begged. Instead, he drove them onward.

They found and explored lands far to the south of everything they had discovered before. The heat, the insects, the storms and the dangerous reefs made the trip a nightmare.

There was gold, but the Indians were violent. Perhaps they had heard about the settlers' cruelty and slave trading farther north. Perhaps they were simply defending their land. Anytime the Spaniards tried to claim, settle, and mine their land, these tribes fought fiercely—and then the rainy season set in. Cristóbal was suffering from malaria.

Two of the ships were lost in storms as they tried to get to Hispaniola. Sea worms had burrowed through the wood of the other two vessels. Weevils had buried themselves in the food, too. The ships were leaking, and the men were starving. The ship finally went aground on an island [modern Jamaica].

Only 116 of the 140 men and boys still survived. They were marooned a hundred miles from Hispaniola. Tainos on the island helped with food, but the men were sick at heart, angry, and ill from the heat. Diego tried to paddle a canoe to La Isabela to get help, but he was attacked by hostile Indians. Next, two canoes were tied together and fitted with a sail. Two Spaniards set out with six Indians for La Isabela. Most of the Indians died. There were not enough left to rescue Cristóbal and his men. The settlers of Hispaniola were in no hurry to send help.

As the months wore on, even the island's Tainos lost patience with Cristóbal's men. They could not understand why the Christians did not bother to grow their own food. They did not try to hunt or to fish, either, and they had long since run out of trinkets to trade. All the strangers seemed to do was take Indian hand-outs and argue.

One year and five days later, a ship arrived to take the survivors back to Spain. There were only a hundred left alive, including Cristóbal and his son. All of them were glad to go home

... fty-three, Cristóbal had arthritis.

He had gout, too, which made it hard to walk. His eyesight was failing, and he suffered horrible fevers.

A month after he got home, Queen Isabella died. Ferdinand, who had never been fond of Cristóbal, now ignored the old captain's pleas for more money. Cristóbal wanted his titles to pass on to his sons. When he made his way by donkey to court, Ferdinand appointed an archbishop to settle Cristóbal's claims. The churchman listened. He decided that the old man should not get any more money than he was already getting. Cristóbal had been a poor leader in the new world. He did not deserve to get any of his titles back. Besides, the archbishop said, Cristóbal had not found a new trade route, after all.

Cristóbal retired to a small house in the south of Spain, where the climate was kind to his aching body. Beatriz and the friars of a nearby monastery took care of him. He had enough income to live comfortably, but his health had failed. It was a sad time. Cristóbal spent his hours thinking back to his days as a hero and his years as a failure.

He died on May 20, 1506.

His sons and his brothers were by his side. Beatriz was with him till the end. His family came to the funeral, but no one from the court bothered to pay their respects to the old explorer.

Cristóbal Colón was buried in Valladolid, Spain. Later, his body was moved to Seville. There are rumors that his body was moved again to Santo Domingo or perhaps to Havana. After five hundred years, nobody knows for sure where Cristóbal's body lies today.

In the fifteenth century, Cristóbal's dream changed the way people saw their world. Suddenly, there were vast unknown continents ~th. People had room now to explore and ~ad new native cultures to explore.

A hundred years passed before Cristóbal and his determined quest began to be celebrated. Slowly he became accepted as a world-famous hero again. Cities, towns, and even whole countries in the New World were named for him. Parades and holidays, statues and universities celebrate his name and accomplishments. English speakers call him Christopher Columbus and named a space shuttle in his honor.

Now, Columbus's reputation is mixed. He brought all of the worst of medieval Europe to the new world: slavery, religious intolerance, disease, and violence. But he also had the radical new idea that he could sail west to get to the Far East. For ten years, he fought for his bold plan. No one believed him. Then he risked his life for this dream across an unknown Ocean Sea. Christopher Columbus was not a good leader, but he was a grand explorer.

A CHRISTOPHER COLUMBUS TIME LINE

(Dates of first forty years are poorly documented.)

BORN, fall of 1451, in Genoa city-state [in modern Italy]

1476—Swims ashore from sinking ship; joins Bartolomo in Portugal.

1477—Sails on merchant ships as far as Guinea and Iceland.

1479—Marries Doña Felipa Perestrello e Moniz.

1480—Son born, Diego.

1484—Presents "The Enterprise of the Indies" to King John of Portugal.

1484—Doña Felipa Perestrello e Moniz dies.

1485—Moves to Spain.

1486—First meeting with Ferdinand and Isabella.

1486—Meets Beatriz Enríques de Arana.

1488—Son born, Fernando.

...dinand and Isabella capture last Moorish ...anada.

VOYAGE 1

1492, April 17—Spanish royalty agrees to finance the Enterprise of the Indies.

1492, August 3—*Pinta, Niña,* and *Santa María* sail from Palos, Spain.

1492, October 12—New World sighted.

1492, October 29—Arrives in Cuba.

1492, November 11—Martin Pinzón deserts, taking *Pinta.*

1492—Arrives in Hispaniola.

1492, December 25—Flagship *Santa María* sinks; Columbus founds La Navidad.

1493, January 6—Pinzón and *Pinta* rejoin Columbus.

1493, January 16—Heads for Spain.

1493, March 4—Arrives in Portugal, arrested.

1493, March 15—Returns to Palos, Spain, in *Niña.*

VOYAGE 2

1493, September—Grand Fleet of seventeen ships leaves Cadiz, Spain.

1493, November 3—Sights island of Dominica at dawn, and, later, Guadeloupe.

1493, November 11—Arrives at Hispaniola.

1493, November 28—Finds Navidad fort destroyed; all settlers killed.

1493, December 8—Founds new colony of La Isabela.

1494, April 30—Lands on Cuba.

1494, May 5—Lands on Jamaica.

1496, March 10—Leaves La Isabela for Spain.

1496, June 8—Returns to Portugal.

VOYAGE 3

1498, May 30—Departs from Spain with four ships.

1498, July 31—Arrives at Trinidad, visits coastline ...agua, Costa Rica, and Panama.

1498, August 19—Arrives at Hispaniola.

1500, October—Arrested and sent home in chains.

VOYAGE 4

1502, May 11—Departs from Spain with four ships.

1502, June 26—Arrives at Santo Domingo, Hispaniola.

1502, July 30—Arrives at the Mosquito Coast (modern Nicaragua).

1503, April 6—Attacked by Indians at Rio Belen; leaves ten days later.

1503, June 25—Ships beached in Jamaica.

1504, June 29—Rescued from Jamaica.

1504, November 7—Columbus returns to Spain.

DIED, May 20, 1506, in Valladolid, Spain.

FOR MORE INFORMATION

Least Heat-Moon, William. *Columbus in the Americas*. New York: Wiley, 2002. This book, written by a Native American, focuses on what happened between the Indians and the Spaniards.

Levinson, Nancy Smiler. *Christopher Columbus: Voyager to the Unknown*. New York: Lodestar/Dutton, 1990.

Meltzer, Milton. *Columbus and the World Around Him*. New York: Franklin Watts, 1990. This book gives a wonderful view of late medieval culture and politics.

Millersville University of Pennsylvania. "Columbus and the Age of Discovery," a computerized information-retrieval system at http://muweb.millersville.edu/~columbus/ Read what they really said. This site links to many original documents from the period of Columbus.

Pelta, Kathy. *Discovering Christopher Columbus: How History Is Invented*. Minneapolis, MN: Lerner, 1991. This is the story of how historians teased out the facts about Columbus from old records—and of how historians work.

★ ★ ★ Childhood of Famous Americans ★ ★ ★

One of the most popular series ever published for young Americans, these classics have been praised alike by parents, teachers, and librarians. With these lively, inspiring, fictionalized biographies—easily read by children of eight and up—today's youngster is swept right into history.

ABIGAIL ADAMS ★ JOHN ADAMS ★ LOUISA MAY ALCOTT ★ SUSAN B. ANTHONY ★ NEIL ARMSTRONG ★ CRISPUS ATTUCKS ★ CLARA BARTON ★ ELIZABETH BLACKWELL ★ DANIEL BOONE ★ BUFFALO BILL ★ ROBERTO CLEMENTE ★ DAVY CROCKETT ★ JOE DIMAGGIO ★ WALT DISNEY ★ AMELIA EARHART ★ THOMAS A. EDISON ★ ALBERT EINSTEIN ★ HENRY FORD ★ BENJAMIN FRANKLIN ★ LOU GEHRIG ★ GERONIMO ★ ALTHEA GIBSON ★ JOHN GLENN ★ JIM HENSON ★ HARRY HOUDINI ★ LANGSTON HUGHES ★ ANDREW JACKSON ★ MAHALIA JACKSON ★ THOMAS JEFFERSON ★ HELEN KELLER ★ JOHN FITZGERALD KENNEDY ★ MARTIN LUTHER KING JR. ★ ROBERT E. LEE ★ MERIWETHER LEWIS ★ ABRAHAM LINCOLN ★ MARY TODD LINCOLN ★ THURGOOD MARSHALL ★ JOHN MUIR ★ ANNIE OAKLEY ★ JACQUELINE KENNEDY ONASSIS ★ ROSA PARKS ★ MOLLY PITCHER ★ POCAHONTAS ★ RONALD REAGAN ★ PAUL REVERE ★ JACKIE ROBINSON ★ KNUTE ROCKNE ★ MR. ROGERS ★ ELEANOR ROOSEVELT ★ FRANKLIN DELANO ROOSEVELT ★ TEDDY ROOSEVELT ★ BETSY ROSS ★ WILMA RUDOLPH ★ BABE RUTH ★ SACAGAWEA ★ SITTING BULL ★ JIM THORPE ★ HARRY S. TRUMAN ★ SOJOURNER TRUTH ★ HARRIET TUBMAN ★ MARK TWAIN ★ GEORGE WASHINGTON ★ MARTHA WASHINGTON ★ LAURA INGALLS WILDER ★ WILBUR AND ORVILLE WRIGHT

★ ★ ★ Collect them all! ★ ★ ★

ALADDIN CLASSICS

ALL THE BEST BOOKS FOR CHILDREN
AND THEIR FAMILIES TO READ!

THE SECRET GARDEN
by Frances Hodgson Burnett
Foreword by E. L. Konigsburg
0-689-83141-2

TREASURE ISLAND
by Robert Louis Stevenson
Foreword by Avi
0-689-83212-5

*ALICE'S ADVENTURES IN
WONDERLAND*
by Lewis Carroll
Foreword by Nancy Willard
0-689-83375-X

LITTLE WOMEN
by Louisa May Alcott
Foreword by Joan W. Blos
0-689-83531-0

THE HOUND OF THE BASKERVILLES
by Sir Arthur Conan Doyle
Foreword by Bruce Brooks
0-689-83571-X

THE WIND IN THE WILLOWS
by Kenneth Grahame
Foreword by Susan Cooper
0-689-83140-4

THE WIZARD OF OZ
by L. Frank Baum
Foreword by Eloise McGraw
0-689-83142-0

*THE ADVENTURES OF
HUCKLEBERRY FINN*
by Mark Twain
Foreword by Gary Paulsen
0-689-83139-0

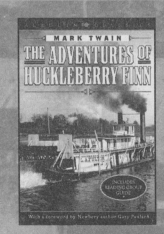